This book belongs to:

....

Written by Abbey Land

Copyright © 2016 B&H Publishing Group, Nashville, Tennessee

BHPublishingGroup.com

978-1-4336-9054-9

Dewey Decimal Classification: C242.62

Subject Heading: DEVOTIONAL LITERATURE/ JESUS CHRIST

Printed in December 2015 in LongGang District, Shenzhen, China

1 2 3 4 5 6 • 20 19 18 17 16

DEVOTIONS
Below the Surface

by
Abbey Land

B&H KIDS

Nashville, Tennessee

Dear Parents,

God has an exciting purpose for your kids' lives, but they might need to look below the surface to discover it. These fifty-two weeks of devotions will encourage kids to submerge themselves in God's Word and discover that Jesus doesn't just see what's on their outsides; He sees the value that's deep inside them. They'll discover how much they are worth to Him, how much they need Him as a Savior, the purpose He has planned for them, and how He loves them no matter what.

Each devotion and each feature (see below) is there to help kids recognize the truth in God's Word and how to apply it in their lives. Are you ready to dive in to an amazing experience? If so, now is the perfect time to discover the truth below the surface!

Think-Deep Question and Answer.
Consider asking your child to provide his or her answer first (maybe even before reading the devotion); then read the devotion and the given answer and talk about it. This discussion will help reaffirm your child's answer and summarize the entire devotion.

Diving Deep into God's Word. To reinforce biblical truths, each devotion includes five verses and discussion questions. Notice these questions often begin with words such as *how* and *why*. By asking questions this way, you can guide your kids to recognize the truth in God's Word and apply it in their lives today.

Chart Your Course. This section offers a variety of experiences from week to week. The simple crafts, activities, or play-together games help your child take in the Think-Deep Question on a more personal level. The whole family can often join in on this part of the devotion experience!

Submerge Yourself in Prayer. Encourage your child to use this prayer as a guide and personalize it. Or if your child struggles with praying aloud, this scripted prayer gives him or her the chance to read the prayer instead.

Chapter 1

Going Below the Surface: Jesus Knows Who I Really Am

While on earth, Jesus encountered many different people—young and old, rich and poor, kind and cruel. No matter what they looked like, acted like, or what other people thought of them, Jesus saw them for who they really were underneath. Did you know Jesus knows who you really are too? Go below the surface and discover what He knows about you and how much He loves you—no matter what!

A Surprising Invitation

When Jesus came to the place, He looked up and said to him, "Zacchaeus, hurry and come down because today I must stay at your house." So he quickly came down and welcomed Him joyfully. All who saw it began to complain, "He's gone to lodge with a sinful man!"—Luke 19:5-7

People did not like him. He was short, and he was rich. He used his job to scare people into giving him money. Do you know the man I'm talking about? Zacchaeus! You may have even sung about him being a "wee little man" when you were little.

Why didn't people like Zacchaeus? Because he collected taxes from them and sometimes took a lot more money from people than was right. He was wealthy, and people knew their money had helped make him rich.

Think-Deep Question of the Week:

Does Jesus love me even though He knows everything about me?

When he heard Jesus was coming to town, Zacchaeus wanted to see Him, so he climbed into a tree to get a better view.

When Jesus saw Zacchaeus, He invited Himself to Zacchaeus's house! People in the crowd could not believe Jesus wanted to go to the house of a man who was a sinner. Everyone knew that Zacchaeus was a sinner, including Jesus.

Do you think Jesus would want to come to your home? The answer is yes! Even though Jesus knows every single thing you have done wrong, He still loves you. No matter what sin you've committed in the past, Jesus wants to spend time with you. Jesus knows who you are deep inside, and He loves you anyway.

Jesus knew you would make mistakes,
and He loves you no matter what you do.

Diving Deep
into God's Word

Luke 19:9-10—Why is it important to know
that Jesus came to save all lost people from their sins?

John 3:17—How does it make you feel to know Jesus came to
save you, not to point out all the wrong things you do?

1 Timothy 1:15-16—What kind of people do you think
Jesus came to save?

Psalm 139:3—How do I know for sure Jesus knows when I sin?

Mark 2:17—Why did Jesus come to earth?

Chart Your Course

1. If you could have anyone visit your home, who would you invite? It could be someone famous, dead or alive, or someone who is special just to you. Ask family members to write down their chosen guests without sharing who it is. (If someone needs to draw a picture, that's fine too!) Collect the pieces of paper and mix them up.

2. Reveal each guest's name and take turns guessing who might have picked each guest to invite. Ask all of your family members to share their reasons for picking each guest.

3. Now imagine Jesus coming to visit you in your home, just like He did with Zacchaeus! Would you be ready? What would you say? Would you act differently than you do now?

4. Talk with your family about the different kinds of people Jesus would visit if He came to your city today. Remember, Jesus came to save everyone, so Jesus would visit anyone!

Submerge Yourself in Prayer

Dear God,
Thank You for loving me no matter what I do, even when I sin. Help me remember to show love to others too. I want to remember that You sent Jesus to save anyone who will follow Him. Amen.

Dealing with Differences

"How is it that You, a Jew, ask for a drink from me, a Samaritan woman?" she asked Him. For Jews do not associate with Samaritans. Jesus answered, "If you knew the gift of God, and who is saying to you, 'Give Me a drink,' you would ask Him, and He would give you living water." —John 4:9-10

Is there someone you don't like to be around? Maybe it's someone who is not very nice or uses bad language; in that case, it might be best not to spend too much time with that person! But other times you might be uncomfortable being around someone just because he or she is different from you. Maybe he speaks a different language or she celebrates a holiday you've never heard of before. Or maybe the person is homeless or old and sick, so you think you don't have anything in common.

In Jesus' time, Jews and Samaritans didn't like each other at all. So when Jesus asked the Samaritan woman for a drink of water in John 4, it was a big deal! Jews and Samaritans did not talk, eat, or hang out together. But Jesus didn't care about those kinds of rules, and He spent

Think-Deep Question of the Week:

How does Jesus want me to treat people who are different from me?

several moments with the woman at the well talking to her about her life. She was amazed at all Jesus knew about her—things no stranger she met at the well should know.

When Jesus asked the woman if she wanted living water, she knew He wasn't talking about something to drink. Jesus said if she took the water He offered, she would never be thirsty again. Then Jesus talked about eternal life with the woman. When she realized Jesus was the Messiah, the one God had promised would come to save her people, she went to share the news with others. Once the people heard what she had to say about Jesus, they believed in Him as well! God used the woman at the well to bring others to Jesus, even though she didn't have the best reputation in her community.

When you deal with people who are different from you, remember that you have one big thing in common with them: you are all loved by Jesus! Even when you know someone is very different from you, you can still show that person His love. Jesus wants you to tell others about Him, just like the Samaritan woman did.

Jesus wants you to follow His example and show love to everyone.

Diving Deep into God's Word

1 John 4:11—Why is it important for you to share Jesus' love with others?

Ephesians 4:32—How might the way you treat others affect what they think about Jesus?

1 Peter 3:8—If you know someone has done things you don't agree with, how should you treat him or her?

Romans 5:8—Why do you think Jesus was kind to all people, not just ones who were doing the right things?

John 4:13-14—What are some things Jesus can offer that no one else on earth can?

Chart Your Course

1. Talk with your family about people in your community who are different from you, especially people who are in need. Who can you think of?

2. Prepare some water bottles or simple snacks to provide to people in your neighborhood or city. Use markers, stickers, and colored paper to decorate the items you choose with simple phrases such as "Jesus loves you."

3. Develop a plan to deliver your snacks and water. You can keep them in the car for the next time you see someone in need, or you and your family could take them to a homeless shelter.

4. Pray for those who will receive your items. Ask God to show them that Jesus loves them no matter what they've done.

Submerge Yourself in Prayer

Dear God,
Thank You for loving me no matter what I've done. Help me show Your love to others. I want others to know about You and Your love.
Amen.

A Sticky Situation

If we confess our sins, He is faithful and righteous to forgive us our sins and to cleanse us from all unrighteousness.—1 John 1:9

Are you kidding me?" Landon asked as he wiped shaving cream off his cheek. His brother Davin had smeared it all over his face while he was sleeping. Landon took off after his brother, prepared to get revenge. Davin barely escaped outside where their mom was working on the garden.

Landon was smart enough to know he shouldn't try to get back at Davin right in front of his mom. He began to plot his plan of attack and headed back into the house, but his mom stopped him.

"What's up with your face? Aren't you a little young to be shaving?" his mom asked. Landon quickly replied, "Davin did this! Can you believe it? I was sleeping, and the next thing I knew I was a sticky mess!"

Landon's mom was doing her best not to laugh. She smiled and asked, "Have you looked in a mirror yet?" Landon shook his head no as his

Think-Deep Question of the Week:

Will Jesus forgive me when I keep messing up?

mom directed him to the bathroom. When he saw himself, Landon couldn't help but laugh. He had a full, white beard! Landon was still mad, but maybe a little less.

He washed his face and then went back outside. Davin was sitting with his mom. He looked at Landon and quietly said, "I'm sorry for putting shaving cream all over your face, even if it was really funny." His mom gave him a serious look, and Davin said, "I'm sorry."

Landon just stood there for a minute, but his mom cleared her throat and he knew what to do. "I forgive you, Davin. Hey, Mom, can we have a shaving cream fight?" His mom replied, "As long as you do it outside, go for it. Don't get it in your eyes!"

Was it easy for Landon to forgive Davin? Probably not. He was mad, and his brother had made a mess. But how many times a day do you think Landon messed up? How about you? Once? Twice? Lots of times? How many times will Jesus forgive you for those mistakes? Every single time you ask. Jesus knows who you are, and He loves you. He doesn't want you to sin, and you should do your best not to. The truth is, though, only Jesus is perfect. You will mess up and get yourself into sticky situations, but Jesus will forgive you when you ask Him to.

You will keep sinning, but Jesus will keep forgiving you when you ask Him to.

Diving Deep into God's Word

Colossians 3:13—Why is it important to forgive others?

Matthew 6:14-15—How does knowing that God forgives you help you forgive others?

Matthew 18:22—When do you think you can quit forgiving others?

Romans 3:23—Who does the Bible say has sinned?

Romans 6:23—What do people who sin deserve, and what does Jesus do instead?

Chart Your Course

1. Cover a table with a disposable tablecloth or wax paper. Spray shaving cream on it and spread it out.

2. Take turns with your family members writing words or drawing pictures of times you may need to ask for forgiveness from one another. Then take your hand and smear away the word or picture. Start over!

3. Spend a few minutes talking about the importance of forgiveness, how difficult it can be to forgive, and how God forgives you and lets you start over.

4. Help clean up the area when you are finished.

Submerge Yourself in Prayer

Dear God,
Thank You for forgiving me when I mess up. Help me forgive others, even when it is hard for me to do.
Amen.

Digging for a Purpose

He made known to us the mystery of His will, according to His good pleasure that He planned in Him for the administration of the days of fulfillment—to bring everything together in the Messiah, both things in heaven and things on earth in Him.—Ephesians 1:9-10

He did it on purpose!" Sarah screamed as she ran toward her parents on the beach while wiping her eyes and crying.

"No, I didn't! It was an accident, I promise!" Spencer responded. "I didn't mean to kick sand in her face. I didn't even know she was sitting there. I was building the biggest sandcastle in the entire world."

Sarah was even more upset by the time she reached her parents. Her mom grabbed a water bottle to rinse out her eyes while Spencer continued to explain what happened. The kids began to argue back and forth until Dad raised his arms and said, "Enough!"

Does it matter if someone hurts you on purpose or accident? Either way it still hurts, right? Saying something has a purpose means there is

Think-Deep Question of the Week:

Does God have a purpose for my life?

a reason behind it. What if your teacher gave you homework but told you that you weren't going to learn anything from it? What if your coach told you to kick the soccer ball a hundred times but it wasn't going to help you play any better? What if a submarine took a dive to the floor of the ocean, but the crew onboard had no assignment when they got there? Purpose is important!

The great news is you don't have to wonder if you have a purpose. You do! God says so right in Ephesians 1:9–10. God's purpose is for you to tell others about Him, learn more about Him, and grow as a Christian. Each person has a purpose, but that doesn't mean each person is fulfilling his purpose. God gives you purpose, and it is your job to carry it out.

On difficult days, confusing days, or sad days, remember God has a specific purpose and plan for you. If you aren't sure you are following God's purpose, pray about it! Ask God for help. He, above anyone else, wants to see you make good choices and follow His plan for your life.

Before you were even born, God had a plan and purpose for your life.

Diving Deep into God's Word

Isaiah 46:10—How do you know you are a part of God's plans to accomplish His purpose?

Romans 8:28—How do you think God is able to work things for His good, no matter what has happened?

Jeremiah 29:11—What kind of purpose do you think God has for you?

Psalm 138:8—What are some things you think God might ask you to do to help you find your purpose?

Isaiah 55:11—How does the Bible help you with your purpose?

Chart Your Course

1. Play a game called "Purpose." Get an empty trash can and seven sheets of paper. Write one letter of the word *purpose* on each piece of paper, and crumple each one into a ball.

2. Take turns attempting to toss a ball into the trash can. After each basket you make, uncrumple the paper. Play until all the letters have been revealed and you spell out the word *purpose*.

3. Talk with your parents about what you think God's purpose is for you. Ask your parents what they think, and spend time praying about how you can remind yourself God has a purpose for you.

Submerge Yourself in Prayer

Dear God,
Thank You for giving me a purpose. I want to make good choices. Help me remember Your purpose for my life.
Amen.

God's Children All Over the World

But to all who did receive Him, He gave them the right to be children of God, to those who believe in His name.—John 1:12

The sounds of excited, energetic kids in beautiful, colorful costumes and music filled the air. Children from the country of Uganda covered the stage with their huge smiles and voices of praise for God. This group of children was traveling the United States, sharing their stories in churches across the country. All the members of the choir came from Uganda, where they lived in a community with other children who had lost their parents.

My family was excited to host three boys and a chaperone from the group. I was nervous too! What if they didn't like the food I made? What if they thought we did strange things? The moment the boys walked in the door, all my worry went away. These boys were polite and friendly, and they ate everything I put in front of them! We talked, played, and

Think-Deep Question of the Week:
Whom does God consider His children?

learned more about each others' lives, how the boys' lives were different from my boys,' and how much all the boys had in common.

On the last night they were at our home, we enjoyed dinner on the screened-in porch overlooking the backyard. In three short days, you could almost mistake us for one big, happy family! I couldn't help but imagine this was what God meant when He called us all children of God.

Our skin colors were different, we spoke different languages, and our backgrounds were different, but you know what we had in common? We all loved God, believed Jesus died on the cross to save us from our sins, and confessed Jesus as Savior and Lord of our lives. Jesus knows who we are.

If you have trusted Jesus as your Savior, you don't have to wonder if you belong anywhere. You belong to God. You are His child, and you are loved.

Those who trust Jesus as their Savior are God's children.

Diving Deep into God's Word

Galatians 3:6—What do you think makes you a child of God?

Romans 8:14—If you are one of God's children, who leads you?

Romans 8:16—Who do you think knows you are a child of God?

Galatians 3:28—When we are children of God, are we on different sides or on one side?

John 1:29—Why did Jesus come to earth?

Chart Your Course

1. With a parent's permission, use a dry erase marker to write the words "I am a child of God" on a mirror in your bathroom or your room.

2. Talk with your parents about why it is important to remember that you belong to God.

3. Challenge your family to come up with other "I am" phrases to add to the mirror when you learn more of them while doing these devotions.

4. Review the devotions you've read so far to discover some other "I am" phrases you can add to the list on your mirror.

Submerge Yourself in Prayer

Dear God,
Thank You for making me Your child. Help me be kind to others. I want others to know I belong to You! Amen.

Looking for the Light

He redeemed my soul from going down to the Pit,
and I will continue to see the light. — Job 33:28

The bottom of the ocean is very dark. As you travel deeper and deeper in the water, your surroundings become more difficult to see. Before you know it, you aren't even able to see your hand in front of your face. Sometimes sin can make you feel like you are all alone in the dark too.

Have you ever told a simple lie, and then a few minutes later, you ended up telling a more complicated lie, just to cover up the simple one? Before you knew it, you weren't even sure what you had said and you couldn't repeat the information exactly like you told it the first time! And in the end, you got in trouble. Your choices matter!

Maybe you had a bad day and you spoke rudely to your parents. Your parents got angry, and you got chores added because of your attitude. Your chores took longer than you expected, and you missed the opportunity to play outside because it was dark when you were done. Do you see how one simple choice can affect everything you do after that?

God chooses to redeem you through the sacrifice of His Son, Jesus. Just because you have been redeemed doesn't mean you will never sin again. Because you are human, you will always be tempted by and give in to sin. But you have the power of forgiveness. Because God has redeemed you through Jesus Christ, you can always be forgiven of your sin. All you have to do is ask, and God will forgive.

In Job 33:28, Job was in a very dark place. His life had been destroyed. His family, home, and livestock had been taken away from him. But this verse shows that Job wasn't ready to give up on God. Even if you feel like you've committed the worst sin in the world and there's darkness all around you like at the bottom of the ocean, you can ask for help. God will redeem you and bring you out of the darkness. You can be set free from your mistakes. All you have to do is ask!

Redemption means to be saved. God redeems you when you ask for forgiveness of your sins.

Diving Deep into God's Word

2 Timothy 3:16—Why is it important to read the Bible to learn about redemption?

Galatians 2:20—Why are you able to be redeemed?

Psalm 107:8—How should you treat God because of His choice to redeem you?

Ephesians 1:7—How does God choose to redeem you?

John 14:6—How many ways can you be redeemed?

Chart Your Course

1. Did you know there are five different ocean zones? (sunlight, twilight, midnight, abyss, and trenches) With your parents' help, do some research about the different zones.

2. Create a picture (using tissue paper, paint, clay, crayons, or different colors of construction paper) to demonstrate the different zones.

3. After you've learned about the different zones, talk with your family about the answer to today's Think-Deep Question. Do you have to work your way through different steps to be redeemed? The ocean has different zones, but God only has one zone, called redemption. All you have to do is ask for it, and God will redeem you!

4. Write the words "I am redeemed" on your art project and display it somewhere in your house as a reminder that God provided a way for us to have redemption through His Son, Jesus.

Submerge Yourself in Prayer

Dear God,
I know I mess up. I know I make mistakes, but I don't want to keep making the same ones. Thank You for redeeming me and saving me from my sins.
Amen.

Free?

> The Spirit's law of life in Christ Jesus has set you free
> from the law of sin and of death.—Romans 8:2

On a vacation with friends and family at the beach recently, I saw an ice-cream shop's sign that said, "Ask us about our free ice cream." When we got inside, we discovered that "free" meant the ice cream didn't have certain things in it, such as sugar, gluten, or artificial flavoring. But we still had to pay for what *was* in the ice cream, so no ice cream was really *free* on that day.

Is anything ever really free? The word *free* can be used in many different ways—as an adjective, an adverb, and a verb. You can *free* a shark from its cage, a fish can swim *freely*, and the crab is *free* to roam on the ocean floor. In Romans 8:2, the verse explains you are free because of Jesus. What kind of free are you?

God allows you the chance to be free from the punishment of sin forever. How much does it cost to be free from death and have eternal life? Nothing! Remember, it is free! How can it be free, though? You can be free in Christ because He sacrificed His life for your freedom. He paid the price for your sin when He died on the cross. What is free to you came at a cost for Jesus and God.

Once you've accepted the free gift of eternal life, you don't ever have to worry about returning the gift. You don't need a receipt, and you don't have to prove you have the gift! How cool is that?

But maybe you don't feel free today. Maybe you are worried because even though you said you were sorry, you still feel guilty about yelling at your little brother. Maybe you are confused about what you believe and you aren't sure if God is okay with your doubt. Maybe you cleaned up the mess you made in the kitchen but you still feel bad that you disobeyed your mom. You can be free from all those things. No "maybe" exists in freedom. Freedom in Christ is a real thing. That's how God designed you to be.

You don't have to worry that God will trick you and make you pay for your sins. Jesus promises you will be free if you choose to believe in Him. Jesus wants you to enjoy the freedom He offers to anyone who will accept the gift.

Jesus died on the cross to free you from your sins. Confess Jesus as your Lord and Savior, ask God to forgive your sins, and He will forgive you.

Diving Deep into God's Word

John 8:32—What do you need to do to realize you've been set free?

John 8:36—If you believe in Jesus, what does that allow you to be?

Romans 7:25—Who has the power to free you from your sin?

Romans 6:22—What does being free from sin allow you to be?

Galatians 5:13—Why do you think God chose to set you free from your sins?

Chart Your Course

1. Plan a family ice-cream date. You can go out for ice cream, or you can buy some at the store and create sundaes at home. Don't forget the sprinkles and chocolate sauce to go on top!

2. Spend your family time *free* from electronics. Ask everyone to put away phones and electronic devices.

3. Talk with your family about your week. Share one of your favorite things you've done this week. Listen to your family members share their answers too.

4. Choose one of the verses from Diving into God's Word, and challenge your family to memorize it. Work together learning the verse and talk about how it is important in your life today.

Submerge Yourself in Prayer

Dear God,
Thank You for setting me free. Help me remember I can't do anything to earn Your love. I want to share with others how to be free.
Amen.

Picking Teams

For He chose us in Him, before the foundation of the world,
to be holy and blameless in His sight.—Ephesians 1:4

Brooks loved playing basketball, and he was good at it too. Whenever it was time to pick teams during PE class, he was always chosen first. Everybody wanted him to play for their team! Brooks was happy everybody wanted him on their team, but picking teams also made him sad. His best friend, Eli, was usually the last to be chosen. It wasn't because people didn't like Eli; he just wasn't the best ball player. Brooks didn't like seeing his friend feel unwanted.

Have you ever been picked last to be on a team? Maybe you weren't chosen to sing in the special music group at church. Or you tried out for a part in a play and someone else got the part. No one wants to feel left out or unwanted, do they? Guess what? You weren't picked last. You are wanted. Check out Ephesians 1:4. What does it say that God did? He chose you! That's right, you were chosen by Him. Not only were you chosen, but He has made you holy. You have been set apart by God. You are His first choice. You don't have to wonder *if* God will choose you for His team, because He already has!

Check out what else God chose you to be—blameless. How often do you stay mad at yourself when you have done something wrong? Blaming yourself can be easy to do. Here in Ephesians 1:4, God makes it known that not only has He chosen you and set you apart, but He is giving you freedom from your sin! All you have to do is ask for forgiveness. When you do, God is able to remove the sin from you. You don't have to carry the blame of your past mistakes. Remember, you are God's first choice!

You don't have to do anything to make God choose you. He always loves you!

Diving Deep into God's Word

Matthew 25:34—How do you think God has chosen to bless you?

John 17:24—When do you think God chose to love you?

2 Thessalonians 2:13—How does knowing God chose you make you feel toward Him?

Colossians 1:22—How are you able to be called "holy" by God?

2 Timothy 1:9—What can you do to earn the right to be called holy by God?

Chart Your Course

1. Play a choices game. Make a list of things to choose from: Oceans or mountains? Submarine or ship? Scuba diving or snorkeling?

2. Invite your family to take turns revealing their personal choices and the reasons for choosing the way they did. For example, your mom may choose to go snorkeling because she doesn't want to dive into deep water.

3. Discuss your different answers and how each of you chose your answers for different reasons.

4. Locate Ephesians 1:4 in your Bible. Write the verse on a note card and circle the words that remind you that God chose you. Remember that Jesus knows you, loves you, and has set you apart to do His work. Put the notecard on your bedside table or someplace you look every day so you can remember that God chose you!

Submerge Yourself in Prayer

Dear God,
Thank You for choosing me. Help me remember that I am important to You. Thank You for loving me even when I mess up. Amen.

A Call for Help

He has rescued us from the domain of darkness and transferred us into the kingdom of the Son He loves. —Colossians 1:13

My family and I were playing on the beach when suddenly, a big wave surprised my sister as she was sitting near the water. Ava fell and began to be carried away by the receding waves. I rushed to rescue her. Thankfully, she wasn't in serious danger, and soon we were all laughing at how my sister managed to fall into the ocean.

Riptides and currents can make for serious situations for swimmers. Water can become dangerous, and lifeguards are not always nearby to help when problems arise. Sometimes even boats get in trouble and need to be rescued from sea. What about you? Do you think you need to be rescued? Think about times you might have gotten into trouble. Maybe you got hurt in a bike wreck or on a playground and needed a bandage, stitches, or even a cast! Perhaps you have needed to be rescued from a situation where friends were watching a movie you knew you shouldn't see. Did you realize you could call your parents for help, or were you worried how they would react?

You do not ever have to wonder who you can call on for help in times of trouble. God reveals a promise He has already made and delivered on in Colossians 1:13. Notice the verse doesn't say, "For those who make all the right choices, God rescued them." God rescues those who want to be rescued. He has given each person on earth the possibility of rescue from the consequences of sin. No one is left behind.

Do you need to be rescued from sin? Call on God for help. God is the ultimate rescuer. When you choose to believe and confess Jesus as your Savior and Lord, consider yourself rescued! God will make you the promise of eternal life spent with Him. Can you imagine a better way to be rescued? If you haven't allowed God to rescue you, ask Him to do so today. Become a part of the kingdom of God, like He so wants you to be.

God has never broken any of His promises.
If God says He will rescue you, He will.

Diving Deep
into God's Word

Isaiah 60:2—How do you think God's glory
compares to the darkness described in the Bible?

Acts 26:18—Why is God's forgiveness seen
as light and sin is called darkness?

Psalm 82:4—How can people be rescued by God?

Job 29:12—Whom will God rescue?

Psalm 72:12—Name some people you think
need to be rescued by God.

Chart Your Course

1. Find a few small waterproof items from around your house. Get an ice cube tray or a few small cups, and place an item or two in each cup. Fill each container with water and place in the freezer until the water has frozen solid.

2. Put a towel on top of a cookie sheet, and place the frozen items on the prepared area. Use different methods to figure out what melts the ice the fastest. You may use salt, hot water, or a plastic spoon to chip away at the ice. The goal is to rescue, or free, the items from the ice.

3. When you've rescued the items, talk about the best method for doing so. As a family, discuss your answers to this week's Think-Deep Question: "How do I know if God will rescue me?"

Submerge Yourself in Prayer

Dear God,
Help me remember the promises You make in the Bible.
Help me remember You always keep Your promises. Thank You for helping me see that I can be rescued from sin.
Amen.

Chapter 2

Searching for Treasure: Jesus Knows My Worth

Scuba divers will travel to the deepest water in search of treasure from sunken boats on the bottom of the sea. What kind of treasure is there to be found? Is it valuable? Are divers able to tell how much a discovery is truly worth just by looking at it? Usually the treasure has to be brought to the surface and studied by experts. But Jesus already knows your worth, no study needed. It's time to dive in to discover what a treasure you are to Jesus!

Sinking Treasure

I chose you before I formed you in the womb; I set you apart before you were born. I appointed you a prophet to the nations.—Jeremiah 1:5

The SS *Gairsoppa* set sail from West Africa for Liverpool, England, in 1941 during World War II with a large load of silver. Sadly, the boat was bombed by a German U-boat off the coast of Ireland and sank into the ocean. And that's where the boat and its treasure stayed—at the bottom of the ocean floor—until 2012. In 2010, a company called Odyssey Marine Exploration was given a contract by the British government to search for and recover the treasure. The wreckage was found, and in 2012, more than forty-nine tons of silver were recovered from the shipwreck. In 2013, they brought up another sixty-one tons! Some people believe it might be the largest shipwreck recovery in history!

How did the company locate the treasure? They used maps, history, and technology to determine where the ship might have sunk. The company

Think-Deep Question of the Week:

What am I worth to God?

knew there was value in locating the wreckage, but they didn't know how *much* value or even if they would find the lost fortune at all!

That lost treasure was worth a great deal to the company and to the government. They spent a lot of time, resources, and money to find it. Did you know that you are worth more to God than all that silver? Do you know how much God values you? Jeremiah 1:5 says God chose you before you were formed! God knew He wanted you before you even breathed your first breath of air. You are His creation! Before your mom or dad got to see you for the first time, God loved you.

Odyssey Marine Exploration planned carefully before they began to search for the ship wreckage. They had to put in hours of studying and work to retrieve the silver from the ocean floor. The company had to earn the money it made. But you do not have to earn your worth with God. You were chosen, loved, and valued by God before you even knew Him. You are worth more to God than one hundred and ten tons of silver!

Diving Deep into God's Word

1 Corinthians 8:3—When you know how much you are worth to God, how should you treat Him?

Galatians 1:15—Why is it important to realize *when* God chose you?

Isaiah 49:1—Why did God think you were important before you were born?

Psalm 139:16—Why are you worth so much to God?

Psalm 119:73—How can you show God that you understand how important you are to Him?

Chart Your Course

1. Did you know that when a company recovers a treasure, it doesn't get to keep it all? An agreement is made before the exploration begins. In the case of the SS *Gairsoppa*, the company got to keep 80 percent and the British government received 20 percent.

2. Ready for a little math? One hundred and ten tons of silver have been recovered from the ship wreckage. Ask your parents to help you figure out how much silver went to the company and how much went to the British government.

3. Count out 110 pennies or cut out 110 small squares of paper. Then separate the items into two piles to represent what the British government and Odyssey Marine Exploration received from the discovery.

4. Now gather your family, and talk about the answer to this week's Think-Deep Question: *What am I worth to God?* Remember, you don't have to search for your worth or earn it. And you don't have to worry about math or fractions when you think about your worth to God!

Submerge Yourself in Prayer

Dear God,
Thank You for teaching me that I mattered before I was even born. Help me remember that I am important to You—more important than the biggest earthly treasure. Help me show others they are important to You too.
Amen.

A Brave Bird

Aren't two sparrows sold for a penny? Yet not one of them falls to the ground without your Father's consent. . . . So don't be afraid therefore; you are worth more than many sparrows.—Matthew 10:29-31

I was visiting my friend Jane in Florida, and I was excited to get to go to the beach to enjoy the sunshine and water. Ever since my friend moved to Florida, she had been telling me the birds there were a little on the wild side. I thought maybe she was being a little dramatic, but I soon learned that wasn't true! My friend and I were sitting on the beach enjoying sub sandwiches when all of a sudden a bird landed in front of me and took a bite of my sandwich—while I was taking a bite from the other end!

I was shocked and didn't know what to do! Then the bird sat right in front of me and ate the bread it had bitten off my sandwich. Jane and

Think-Deep Question of the Week:

How much do I matter to God?

I had a great visit, and I will never forget those crazy birds. God had a funny way of making sure that bird was well fed!

According to Matthew 10:29–31, you are worth way more to God than a wild bird on a beach in sunny Florida! God cares about you and knows everything about you. He made you, after all! You matter to God, and you never have to worry about being forgotten by God. He loves you more than anything else in all of creation, and He will take care of you. God always has time for you, is always willing to listen to you, and always loves you!

You matter more to God than anything else
He created!

Diving Deep into God's Word

Matthew 6:26—Why do you think God used birds
as an example to help you understand your worth?

Matthew 12:12—Why do you think God mentions another
animal—a sheep—to explain how valuable you are to Him?

Luke 12:24—What are some things God provides for you and your
family that He doesn't provide for other creatures He created?

Job 35:11—Who did God put in charge of caring for
the animals? Why do you think He did that?

Psalm 50:11—How does it make you feel to
know how much you matter to God?

Chart Your Course

1. Create a simple bird feeder with your family.

2. Thread grapes and whole-grain round cereal on a piece of craft wire. Shape it into a circle, choose a tree or pole to hang it on, and twist the two ends together. You could also make one by covering an apple or empty paper towel roll in peanut butter, rolling it in birdseed, and using yarn to attach it to a branch or pole.

3. Watch the feeder to see how many birds or squirrels snack on your tasty treat. Think about all the ways God cares for His creation.

Submerge Yourself in Prayer

Dear God,
Thank You for reminding me how much You care for me. Help me remember I matter to You more than any of the other wonderful things You created!
Amen.

A Puppet Presentation

You are precious in My sight and honored, and I love you.
—Isaiah 43:4

When I was in high school, I joined a puppet ministry at my church. We would travel around performing for children who may not have ever heard about how much God loved them. One of the songs we would sing was "Jesus Loves the Little Children," a favorite from when I was little. No matter how tired my hand would get from holding that puppet, reminding the kids they were precious to God was always a joy.

Do you know the "Jesus Loves the Little Children" song? The chorus goes like this: "Jesus loves the little children, all the children of the world. . . . They are precious in His sight. Jesus loves the little children of the world."

What exactly does the word *precious* mean? It means that something is of very great value. Things that are considered precious aren't to be

Think-Deep Question of the Week:
How does God see me?

wasted. You may only have a precious amount of drinking water left for the rest of your camping trip, or precious stones may have been discovered in a deep cave. The word is used to describe something that matters and is important.

In Isaiah 43:4, God is speaking directly to you, and He says, "You are precious in My sight." The Creator of the universe is calling *you* valuable. You matter to God just because He made you and you belong to Him, not because of anything you have done. How can you put a price tag on that kind of love? You can't, because it is worth more than anyone could ever pay.

Diving Deep into God's Word

Exodus 19:5—How does it make you feel to know God treasures you?

Isaiah 49:5—What are some things you think God has given you because you are precious to Him?

Deuteronomy 7:6—How do you feel about God calling you one of His chosen people?

Acts 10:34-35—Does God show favoritism?

Matthew 19:14—How did Jesus treat children who wanted to be near Him?

Chart Your Course

1. Find a shoebox, an empty tissue box, or any other container that would make a cool treasure chest.

2. Decorate the box with markers, stickers, and plastic jewels. With the help of an adult, you can even spray paint it gold.

3. Write a few verses, such as those found in Diving into God's Word, on index cards and place them in your treasure chest.

4. Discuss with your family when and why you may need reminders of how God feels about you. As you go through the rest of the devos and read verses that you want to remember, add them to the box.

Submerge Yourself in Prayer

Dear God,
Thank You for caring so much for me. Help me remember that You love me and that I am important to You.
Amen.

What Does the Sheep Say?

Acknowledge that Yahweh is God. He made us, and we are His—His people, the sheep of His pasture.—Psalm 100:3

What does a sheep say?" Nash asked his little brother, Tuck. He was trying to help his brother learn the different sounds each animal makes. After Tuck responded with a *baaa*, Nash turned to his mom and asked, "Mom, why did my Sunday school teacher tell me that God calls us sheep in the Bible?"

Nash's mom smiled and answered, "Great question! I can see why that might sound a little strange to you. Do you know what a shepherd does?"

Nash nodded his head. "A shepherd is someone who takes care of sheep. He keeps the sheep together and tries to keep them from getting hurt or lost or attacked by other animals."

"Exactly!" said Nash's mom. "God uses sheep as an example of how He protects and guides those who believe in Him."

Think-Deep Question of the Week:
Why does God compare me to a sheep?

Nash thought for a minute and then said, "So, God calls us sheep because He wants us to understand how He takes care of us."

Nash's mom gave him a big smile. "You got it! God talks about people as sheep in many places in the Bible. God wants us to remember that He loves us very much and He is always watching over us. God wants us to trust Him and follow Him because He wants to keep us safe."

"Thanks for helping me, Mom. I think I understand it better now. Who knew I was a sheep?" Then Nash and Tuck went back to playing the animal game. Nash said, "Hey, Tuck, if we're all sheep, no wonder you know what the sheep says!"

Think-Deep Answer of the Week:

We are the Good Shepherd's sheep,
and He will take care of us!

Diving Deep into God's Word

Psalm 79:13—Why do people who believe in God
call themselves sheep in the pasture?

Isaiah 40:11—Thinking about God as your Shepherd,
what are some things He does for you?

Matthew 25:32-33—How does it make you feel
to know you are one of God's sheep?

Isaiah 53:6—How is God like a shepherd in your life?

Matthew 18:12—Why do you think God would
go after someone who is lost?

Chart Your Course

1. Play a game of animal charades. Write or draw the following animals on small pieces of paper: *bird, goat, camel, donkey, lion, monkey,* and *sheep.*

2. Fold the pieces of paper and put them in a bowl. Take turns as a family pulling out a paper and acting out the animal for others to guess.

3. Discuss with your family some characteristics of sheep. If you don't know much about sheep, ask your parent to help you do some research.

4. Read the verses from Diving into God's Word to discover how God uses sheep to describe His people.

Submerge Yourself in Prayer

Dear God,
Thank You for making me one of Your sheep. Help me remember You are there to guide me. I want to remember to listen to You and follow You, my Shepherd!
Amen.

A Very Hairy Situation

> Indeed, the hairs of your head are all counted.
>
> —Luke 12:7

Have you ever gotten a bad haircut? You know, you go in thinking your hair is going to look amazing. Then the next thing you know, it looks awful! What happened? One time my children got super short haircuts. I was shocked when they walked out of the salon. I am embarrassed to admit it, but I cried! Who cries over a haircut? It happens a lot more than you think!

Right now, it is estimated that over seven billion people live on earth. The average amount of hair follicles on a person's head is about 150,000. You could use these numbers to try to figure out how many strands of hair are in the world, but I'm not that good at math! Plus, not everyone has exactly 150,000 hair follicles, so that's just an estimate. The possibility of figuring out exactly how many strands of hair are in the world isn't

Think-Deep Question of the Week:

Does God really know everything about me?

looking good. But what does Luke 12:7 say about hair? God knows how much hair is on everyone's head, which means He knows *exactly* how much hair is on your head! Whoa.

Why does it even matter if God knows how many hairs are on your head? Because He wants you to know that He knows everything about you. A few devotions ago, you read about how God cares for you more than He cares for anything else in the world. Why does God keep reminding you how He feels about you? God wants you to be certain of your value to Him. He knows your worth, and you matter to God. You never have to worry or question if God cares for you. God knows everything you think, say, and do, and He loves every big and little part of you.

God made you, and He knows every big
and little thing about you.

Diving Deep
into God's Word

Matthew 10:30—Why do you think God
reminds you in more than one place that He
knows how much hair you have?

Matthew 6:8—Does God know when you need His help?

Genesis 1:27—Why is it important to realize
you were made in God's image?

Psalm 121:7—How does it feel to know God wants
to take care of you?

Mark 10:14—Does God only have time
to listen to adults?

Chart Your Course

1. Attempt to count the hair on one of your family member's head.

2. How long did it take before you became frustrated or gave up on the task? God doesn't have to take time to count anyone's strands of hair. He already knows!

3. Choose one of the verses from Diving into God's Word to write on a card, and place it on the mirror you use when you fix your hair. If you have a brush or comb with a large enough area, ask your parents to help you write a verse in permanent marker on it.

4. Challenge yourself to read the verse whenever you are unsure about what may happen in the future.

Submerge Yourself in Prayer

Dear God,
Thank You for knowing every single detail about my life and still loving me. Thank You for caring about me.
Amen.

A Wonderful Work

You knit me together in my mother's womb. I will praise You because I have been remarkably and wonderfully made. Your works are wonderful, and I know this very well.—Psalm 139:13-14

Name three things you like about yourself." I challenged the girls in my Sunday school class to do this as part of our lesson one day. Most of the girls gave lots of answers very quickly, but one didn't say anything at all. She sat there quietly, probably hoping no one would notice she hadn't answered. I quickly wondered what I should do. *Do I ignore her and pretend I don't realize she isn't saying anything, or should I ask her what she thinks?*

Sometimes even teachers aren't sure what the right thing to do is. After a quick prayer for help, I went over to the quiet girl and put my arm around her. I didn't give her a chance to speak. Instead, I began to share things I liked about her, and as I did, her face started to change.

Think-Deep Question of the Week:

How do I know I was created exactly the way God wanted me to be?

Finally, she gave me a huge smile. I sure was glad to see how happy those words made her!

What three things do you like the most about yourself? Are you struggling to come up with that many things, or is your list already full? Either way, Psalm 139:13–14 is for you. God created you. He made you! And according to this verse in Psalms, everything God makes is wonderful. Guess what you are? One of His works!

You may not like the shape of your nose, how tall or short you feel standing next to your friends, or the fact you are allergic to fish! But each of one those characteristics is part of what makes you, you. God made you who you are, and you can praise God for designing you to be you!

Diving Deep into God's Word

Psalm 92:5—Why is it important to realize that God made great things and that you are one of those great things?

Psalm 111:2—How does God want you to treat what He has created (including yourself!)?

Genesis 1:27—Why do you think God created you in His image?

Genesis 1:31—What did God think about everything He created?

Ephesians 3:9—Why does the Bible mention in several different places that God created everything, including you?

Chart Your Course

1. Write each family member's name on a piece of paper.

2. Pass around the pieces of paper and challenge your family members to write two things they like about each one of you.

3. Take turns reading aloud the compliments, and try to guess which person wrote which compliment.

4. Discuss how easy or difficult it was to think of nice things to say about others. Would it have been more difficult to write things down about yourself?

5. Ask your family to read this week's Bible verse (Psalm 139:13–14) together as a prayer to God.

Submerge Yourself in Prayer

Dear God,
Thank You for making me who I am. Help me remember that everything You make is wonderful!
Amen.

Dangerous

The LORD your God is with you, the Mighty Warrior who saves. He will take great delight in you; in his love he will no longer rebuke you, but will rejoice over you with singing.—Zephaniah 3:17 NIV

Four-year-old Drake loved spending time in the ocean. Jumping waves was his favorite! He had been playing in the water for a long time. He knew it was time to leave because his dad had said it so many times. Drake couldn't help it, though; it was his last day at the beach, and he didn't want to go.

"Daddy!" Drake cried as his dad pulled him out of the water. "I'm not finished yet!"

"Son, I have told you several times that we were leaving soon and gave you a five-minute warning. The water is getting rougher, and you are getting tired. Staying in the waves would be dangerous. I'm only doing what's best for you." Drake was so tired he didn't argue with his dad.

Think-Deep Question of the Week:

How does God feel about me even though He knows I'm a sinner?

Instead, he began to cry. Drake's daddy could have yelled at him and gotten really angry. But you know what he did instead?

Drake's dad began to sing him one of his favorite worship songs. For a moment, Drake continued to cry; then he began to settle down and listen to his dad sing. When his dad finished the song, he looked down and noticed Drake had fallen asleep.

Drake's dad could have chosen to punish his son, but instead he chose to praise God for Drake. Your heavenly Father does the same for you. As a Christian, even when you make a mistake or poor choice, God still rejoices over you (Zephaniah 3:17 says He will even rejoice over you with singing!). God knows everything about you, remember? And He loves you anyway. God wants you to follow His ways and His commands, but there will be times you choose to disobey. God won't be happy when you disobey, but nothing you can do will ever change how much He loves you.

Think-Deep Answer of the Week:

No matter what you say or do,
God loves you.

Diving Deep into God's Word

Isaiah 62:5—Why do you think God
will rejoice over you?

Jeremiah 32:41—Why does doing good make
God want to rejoice?

Deuteronomy 30:9—How does knowing God loves
you no matter what make you feel?

Isaiah 65:19—Why is it important for you
to know you make God glad?

Micah 7:18—Why is it good to know
God doesn't hold on to anger?

Chart Your Course

1. Make a list of ten emotions, such as *happy*, *excited*, *scared*, *angry*, *sad*, or *surprised*. Write each emotion on a separate index card.

2. Mix the cards up in a bowl. Take turns drawing a card out of the bowl and making a face to represent that emotion. See if the rest of the family can guess which emotion is showing on your face. You might have to work hard at it!

3. When you've acted out all ten emotions, talk with your family about which ones were easy to show on your face and which ones were easy to guess.

4. Now talk about how it feels to see people you love when they are sad versus when they are happy, when they are angry versus when they are peaceful. No matter what, you still love those people, right? It's the same with God. Whether we are joyful or angry, whether we make good choices or bad choices, God still loves us.

Submerge Yourself in Prayer

Dear God,
Thank You for loving me even though I am a sinner. Help me remember that there is nothing that I can do that will make You love me any less.
Amen.

Looking Underneath

"Man does not see what the LORD sees, for man sees what is visible, but the LORD sees the heart."—1 Samuel 16:7

The glaciers were everywhere I turned. I couldn't escape them. In the middle of the summer, I was wearing a coat and I was still a little cold! I was on a boat in the middle of Glacier Bay in Alaska. Nothing could have prepared me for the amazing beauty of the large bodies of ice in front of me. While I was admiring the view, a huge piece of ice fell off one of the glaciers and tumbled into the ocean. It was fascinating to watch as the iceberg began to float away.

One type of iceberg is called a growler. The part of the iceberg you can see floating in the water looks about the size of a large truck, but beneath the surface it is much larger and potentially dangerous to ships passing by. If you were to judge the growler iceberg only by what you could see above the water, you wouldn't be judging accurately, would you?

Think-Deep Question of the Week:

What does Jesus know about me that no one else knows?

With advanced technology, ships can be prepared and identify these icebergs because they know there is more underneath than what they can see.

Just like there is more to a growler under the water's surface, there's more to you than what people see. Thank goodness Jesus sees more than what shows on the outside! He sees your heart, and that is a good thing! Many times people only see or recognize your mess-ups, your failures, or your mistakes. But Jesus knows what you are thinking, feeling, dreaming, and hoping. He knows your insides and your outsides. In fact, God misses nothing! Nothing surprises Him. God sees every part of you just like a sailor using radar can see the iceberg under the surface. Even when you think no one else really knows you or understands you, you can trust that God knows your heart. He knows all about you, and He knows how much you love Him and want to know Him better.

People may know some parts of you, but Jesus knows everything about you and your heart!

Diving Deep into God's Word

Luke 16:15—Why is it better that God really knows your heart instead of people knowing it?

John 8:15—What is the difference between how other people see you and how God sees you?

Romans 8:27—When you experience difficult times in your life, how does it help to trust that God knows your heart?

1 Chronicles 28:9—How does it feel to know you can seek God and that you will find Him when you do?

Proverbs 21:2—Why is it important to remember God knows you better than anyone?

Chart Your Course

1. Get an ice cube tray or small disposable cups to use to create paint. Place water in the tray or cups and then use fruit juice or food coloring to dye the water different colors.

2. Put the containers of water in the freezer. Wait about thirty minutes and then place a wooden craft stick, disposable straw, or plastic spoon in each container to serve as a handle. Place the containers back in the freezer until water is completely frozen.

3. Allow the ice to sit in room temperature a few minutes before removing the ice paints.

4. Use the ice to paint a heart or another picture on heavy-weight paper. As you paint, think about the icebergs and how God knows even the hidden parts of your heart.

Submerge Yourself in Prayer

Dear God,
Thank You for caring about who I am and who I want to be. Help me remember You know me best of all, and You love me.
Amen.

Week 18

Diving Lesson

But when the goodness and loving kindness of God our Savior appeared, he saved us, not because of works done by us in righteousness, but according to his own mercy, by the washing of regeneration and renewal of the Holy Spirit—Titus 3:4-5 ESV

Grayson stood at the end of the diving board and took a few moments to focus. He could feel the eyes of the crowd, waiting for the final dive of the tournAmen.t. So far, he had let his teammates down with two disappointing dives. But this was his chance to prove himself to the team. *I need to show them that I deserve to be here,* he thought to himself. One last breath, and he was off the board.

A few seconds later, it was all over, and Grayson had just completed one of his worst dives ever. He had let his team down. He dried off and made his way silently to the locker room to face his teammates.

Ethan met him at the door. "Tough night out there, Grayson. Shake it off. We'll work even harder next year."

Then Dillon chimed in, "Need a ride to the after-party, Grayson? We've got room in our car."

Think-Deep Question of the Week:

How do my actions affect my worth to God?

"I can't believe you guys are even talking to me," said Grayson, looking surprised. "After all, I just lost the tournAmen.t for you. I'm sure you're ready to kick me off the team."

"What? Nah. We win as a team and we lose as a team," said Dillon. "You already earned your spot when you were chosen to be one of us. So now we stick together. Next time, it might be one of us having a bad night."

Have you ever felt like Grayson? Like you had to earn the right to be part of the team? Or maybe you tried to convince someone to love you or be friends with you. It can be hard.

Maybe you feel the same way about God. Do you ever find yourself doing things to earn God's love and feel important to Him? Maybe you aren't sure He will love you, so you pray every night and go to church so God doesn't forget about you. Here's the good news: God loves you and sent His Son, Jesus, to earth to save you. He is happy when you serve him and make good choices, but there's nothing you can do to earn the reward of eternal life in heaven. Before you stepped one foot on this earth, God had already decided to send His Son to die on the cross for you. Nothing you can say or do changes what God has done. And if you trust Jesus as your Savior, you will spend eternity with Him. You are part of God's team!

You cannot earn God's love through doing things. God already loves you!

Diving Deep into God's Word

Ephesians 2:4—Why did God send Jesus to die for your sins?

Ephesians 2:8-9—Why can't you earn your way into heaven?

2 Timothy 1:9—When do you think God determined your worth?

2 Corinthians 11:30—How do you think God feels about people boasting or bragging about what they have done?

Romans 3:28—What do you have to do to realize you can't earn your way into heaven?

Chart Your Course

1. Make a list of things people might think will help them earn God's love.

2. Review the list and draw a line through ideas that are not true.

3. Now make a list of things people can do that would bring honor and glory to God.

4. Use a snorkel (or cardboard tube) to hold up to your mouth while you say each item on the second list of things that are pleasing to God. Let your family members guess what you are saying.

5. Discuss your answer to today's Think-Deep Question.

Submerge Yourself in Prayer

Dear God,
Thank You for loving me. Help me help others realize they don't have to earn Your love. Let my actions show others more about Your love.
Amen.

Chapter 3

Supplying the Submarine: Jesus Knows I Need a Savior

Before a submarine crew heads underwater for several months, they do a lot of planning to make sure they have everything they need, such as food, water, and a way to get rid of garbage! Now think about this—when is the last time you had to remind Jesus of one of your needs? The answer is *never* because He knows your every need already! Grab your scuba gear, and let's head beneath the surface to discover the ways Jesus knows and meets all your needs.

What Did You Say?

"For God loved the world in this way: He gave His One and Only Son, so that everyone who believes in Him will not perish but have eternal life."—John 3:16

How's your hearing? One time I went with a friend when she was having a hearing test. Maggie was worried that she might be going deaf. She was always asking her friends, including me, to repeat what we said to her. She came out of the hearing test with a small smile on her face, and I knew it meant good news. I asked, "So, what did the doctor say?"

Maggie looked embarrassed and told me, "The doctor said my hearing is fine, but my listening skills are poor. I don't have a hearing problem, but I do have a paying-attention problem." My friend and I laughed. Maggie could hear what people were saying to her just fine; she was just choosing not to pay attention and hear what was being said.

Think-Deep Question of the Week:

Why do I need Jesus as my Savior and Lord?

Listening can be difficult for lots of people. Sometimes we hear something so often that we forget to listen to what is being said. For example, I bet you've heard John 3:16 lots of times. It's a popular Bible verse; you might even have it memorized! But when is the last time you really listened to what the verse says? This verse is telling you that God sacrificed His Son because sinners like you and me needed help. God chose to give His Son's life so we wouldn't have to suffer for eternity for our sins.

Everyone needs Jesus. To have eternal life and live in heaven when you die, you must believe that Jesus died on the cross and rose from the grave. You must confess Jesus as your Savior and Lord. Life is better with Jesus. Aren't you glad you listened to that message? It's definitely worth hearing.

You need Jesus as Your Savior because He died to save you from your sins and offer you eternal life.

Diving Deep into God's Word

John 3:36—What does God promise to anyone who believes in Him?

John 6:40—Who can become a Christian?

Romans 5:8—Why do you think Jesus chose to die for you when He knew you would continue to sin?

Romans 8:32—If God gave His Son to die for you even though you were going to keep sinning, how do you think God feels about you?

1 John 4:9—How do you explain God's love to people who don't know Him yet?

Chart Your Course

1. Play a "Name Game" by allowing one family member to choose a letter of the alphabet. Next, each family member must think of someone they know whose name begins with that letter. Allow each family member to say a name until one player cannot think of a name that hasn't already been said.

2. Play a few rounds of the Name Game using different letters.

3. Think about the people you named in the game. Which of them need a Savior? Why?

4. Discuss with your family today's Think-Deep Question. Talk about why everyone needs Jesus as Savior and Lord.

Submerge Yourself in Prayer

Dear God,

Thank You for providing for my biggest need. Thank You for giving me something I don't deserve—eternal life with You. Give me the courage to talk to others about how to become a Christian. Amen.

Dinner Plans

"So don't worry, saying, 'What will we eat?' or
'What will we drink?' or 'What will we wear?' For the idolaters
eagerly seek all these things, and your heavenly Father
knows that you need them."—Matthew 6:31-32

What's for dinner tonight, Mom?" asked Gavin.

"Gavin, really? We are just finishing lunch and you already want to know what's next?"

"Mom, I can't help it! I'm a growing boy! I need fuel for my body to keep it running. I've got soccer practice tonight, and I need energy to play well," responded Gavin with a grin.

Gavin's mom smiled and said, "We're having fish. I found a new recipe I want to try out, and your dad just brought home a load of catfish."

Think-Deep Question of the Week:

What basic needs does God promise to provide for me?

Was Gavin worried that his mom wasn't going to have enough food to feed him dinner? No. Was Gavin's mom worried about having food to feed the family? It doesn't sound like it, does it?

Gavin and his mom weren't worried about where their next meal was coming from, and you shouldn't worry either. Matthew 6:31–32 reminds you that God created you and you shouldn't worry about food and clothing. Why? Because He knows you need these things, and He is in control of all things. God not only knows your needs, He gave you your needs for a reason. Whatever happens to us has meaning because God uses it to grow us. Instead of trusting in our food or clothing, we need to trust in God, in His ways, and in His timing.

God tells you not to worry about what you will eat or what you will drink. When you need something, trust that He is in control.

Diving Deep into God's Word

Psalm 111:5—When do you think God will quit providing for your needs?

Matthew 6:25—Why doesn't God want you to worry about what you are going to wear, eat, or drink?

Matthew 6:27—Why does God say not to worry? How does worrying hurt you?

Philippians 4:6—What do you think God wants you to do when you start to worry about food and clothes too much?

1 Peter 5:7—Why does God provide you food, drink, and clothing?

Chart Your Course

1. Do you know what an acronym is? It's when you take the letters to a word and come up with a different word or phrase for each letter to help you remember the word.

2. Use the letters that spell out the word *worry* to come up with ways to stop or deal with worry when it begins to happen. For example, you might decide when you begin to worry that you should take a **W**alk. Or maybe if you're worried about what to eat, you should just **O**rder pizza!

3. Write down the different ideas you come with on a piece of paper and place it where the family will see it: on the fridge, on the inside of a cabinet door, or in the pantry.

4. Discuss with your family how it makes you feel to know God already knows what you need and wants to provide it for you.

Submerge Yourself in Prayer

Dear God,
Thank You for knowing what I need and providing it for me. When I begin to worry about things like what I'm going to eat or what I'm going to wear, remind me that You are in control! Amen.

Asking for Permission

"If you then . . . know how to give good gifts to your children, how much more will your Father in heaven give good things to those who ask Him!"—Matthew 7:11

Why can't I swim with the dolphins with all my friends when we go to the beach?" Lydia asked her mom as they walked in the door from school.

Lydia's mom was confused. "When did you ask me to go?"

"Just now, Mom," Lydia said, getting a little frustrated that her mom didn't understand the question.

As patiently as she could, Lydia's mom said, "Honey, you just said, 'Why can't I go swimming with dolphins with all my friends?' That isn't asking me if you can go; you asked why you can't go."

Lydia scrunched up her nose and thought about it. Then she said, "Oh, yeah, I see what you mean. So, can I go swim with dolphins with my friends?"

Think-Deep Question of the Week:
What does God promise to give you when you ask?

Mom smiled and said, "Nice try. Why don't you get me some more information, and we'll talk about it."

Why do you think Lydia asked her mom that question in the first place? Did it confuse you as much as it did Lydia's mom? Lydia was setting herself up for disappointment before her mom even knew what Lydia was asking about!

You don't have to worry about being disappointed when you ask God for something. Matthew 7:11 says that if what you ask for is in God's plan, He will provide it for you. God loves to give you good things! Just like Lydia's mom will make the best decision for Lydia based on her safety, God will always make the best decisions for you based on His plan for your life. Don't be afraid to ask Him. Anytime you pray and ask God for something, He promises that He hears you!

God promises to give good things to those who ask Him.

Diving Deep into God's Word

James 1:17—What kind of gifts has God given you when you've asked Him?

Proverbs 28:20—Why do you think God wants to give you good things?

Psalm 139:3—What are some reasons God might not give you what you are asking for, even if it seems like a good thing to you?

Psalm 85:12—What are some good things God gives to everyone?

Psalms 104:28—How do you feel when God gives you gifts?

Chart Your Course

1. Find a gift box, an empty container, or a gift bag. Get a piece of paper, a marker, and scissors.

2. Cut the piece of paper into one-inch strips.

3. On one half of the strips write down gifts God has given you. On the other half write down a few things you are asking God for in your prayer time.

4. Place all the slips of paper in your container. During your devotional time, draw out a slip of paper. If you choose a gift you've already been given, thank God for that gift. If you select a gift you are asking for, spend time in prayer talking to God about it.

Submerge Yourself in Prayer

Dear God,
Thank You for the good things You've given me. Help me remember it is okay to ask for the things I need and want. I know You promise to listen to my prayers.
Amen.

Wish Lists

You do not have because you do not ask.
—James 4:2

Heather couldn't wait to open her birthday presents at her party. She had wanted an underwater camera to take on her family's vacation for months. She had studied catalogs and knew which one she wanted. When she opened up the last gift and it wasn't a camera, she realized she wasn't going to get one. Heather was disappointed, but she tried not to let it show.

After all her friends had gone home, Heather helped her mom clean up. Heather's dad could tell something was bothering her. "Heather, why are you so sad? You just had a great party with all your friends!"

Heather didn't want to say because she was worried her dad would get mad. Finally, though, she explained, "I really wanted an underwater camera to take pictures on our summer vacation, but I didn't get one."

Think-Deep Question of the Week:

Why do I need to ask God for things when He already knows what I want?

Heather's mom and dad both looked confused. Her mom replied, "Honey, did you ever tell anyone you wanted a camera?"

Heather thought for a minute, then realized she hadn't told anyone at all! "I can't believe it! I didn't! I was so busy figuring out which one I wanted that I never even told you about it!"

Heather's dad laughed and then said, "Well, the good news is your grandmother gave you money. I bet if you combine that with the money you've been saving, you'll have enough to buy that camera!"

Have you ever experienced a disappointment like Heather's? Our parents can't read our hearts and minds to know what we want, but guess what? God can. And not only that, He knows what we need. But God still wants you to talk to Him and tell Him the things you want, like if you want help to be a better sibling, or you wish you could go on a special trip with your friends, or even about your wish list for your birthday. God isn't always going to give you what you want, because He knows what is best for you and He has an awesome plan for you. But God is always excited to hear from you, and He wants you to trust that He will answer your prayers in the way that is best!

God already knows what you want and need,
but He loves it when you to talk to Him.

Diving Deep
into God's Word

Jeremiah 29:12—What does God promise
He will do when we pray?

Psalm 145:18—When we pray, where is God?

Matthew 7:7—What happens when you ask God for something?

Matthew 6:6-8—Do you have to go to a specific place to
pray? Or can you pray no matter where you are?

James 1:5—How do you figure out
what your needs really are?

Chart Your Course

1. Play a game of "Father, May I?" with your family. If you have friends visiting, invite them to join in!

2. Choose one person to be the "Father" and stand at the end of the room. The remaining players stand on the other end and must ask permission from the "Father" to take steps toward "him." Each player takes turns asking to take a certain number of steps and what kind of steps, such as tiny, large, or jumps. For example, "Father, may I take three tiny steps?" Each time a player asks, the "Father" must decide if the player can move. Once someone reaches the "Father," the game is over. If a player does not ask permission correctly, he isn't allowed to take the steps.

3. Play the game several times with different "Fathers." Then talk about the game. Was it difficult to remember to ask for permission?

4. Discuss with your family some needs to talk with God about. Talk about how special it is that we can talk directly to God our Father anytime we want—no permission needed!

Submerge Yourself in Prayer

Dear God,
Sometimes I don't understand why I need to pray when You already know what I need and what I want. Help me to remember that You still want me to talk to You. It's an honor to be able to tell You things and ask for Your help!
Amen.

Steering Away from Temptation

No temptation has overtaken you except what is common to humanity. God is faithful, and He will not allow you to be tempted beyond what you are able, but with temptation He will also provide a way of escape that you are able to bear it. —1 Corinthians 10:13

Dawson's family was visiting a naval museum, and their tour guide led them inside an old submarine. The guide cautioned the group not to touch any of the dials, knobs, or equipment, but Dawson was fascinated! He had never seen so many buttons and levers in his entire life! And there was even a large, round steering wheel. He thought no one would notice if he pulled just one lever. As he reached out to touch it, the tour guide turned to him and said, "Thanks for pointing that out for me, friend! I wanted to make sure everyone saw this."

That was close! Dawson was glad the tour guide had seen him and kept him from disobeying. Soon he learned tons of fascinating things about the submarine. And he hadn't broken any of the rules.

Think-Deep Question of the Week:

How does God help me when I'm tempted to do things I shouldn't?

Have you ever been tempted to do something you knew was wrong? What kinds of thoughts went through your head? Did you think about the possible consequences and wonder if it was worth it? You will always be faced with temptations—to lie, to cheat on a test, to do what the popular kids are doing but you know is wrong, and more. Is there a chance no one will ever find out what you did wrong? Sometimes, yes. But God still cares what you do, and He always knows everything.

The truth is all people are tempted, even parents and preachers and Bible-class teachers! The difference is how you respond to the temptation: do you give in or walk away? The good news is God promises to give you a way out. Go back and read the very last sentence of 1 Corinthians 10:13. God provides you with the strength to say no. He can do this is many different ways. In Dawson's situation, a distraction from the tour guide helped him obey the directions he was given. You might resist your next temptation because of a friend's encouragement, a Bible verse you remember, by thinking about a possible consequence, or by trusting that God wants the very best for you. When you are tempted to disobey, remember you can always ask God for help and He will always give it.

Think-Deep Answer of the Week:

God provides you with the strength to say no to temptation.

Diving Deep into God's Word

Matthew 26:41—Why is it easy to be tempted to do wrong?

1 Chronicles 29:17—Why is it good to resist temptation?

James 1:13—According to the Bible, why is it wrong to blame God for tempting you?

1 Peter 4:12—Why should you not be surprised when you face temptation?

1 Timothy 6:9—What are some ways people are tempted?

Chart Your Course

1. Work with your family to make a list of temptations people face. You can be specific and list things such as cheating on a test, lying, gossiping, or eating twelve cookies when your mom told you not to.

2. Ask each family member to take five pieces of paper and write the numbers 1 through 5 on them (one number on each piece of paper).

3. Choose someone to read aloud each temptation on your list, and invite all your family members to rate how much of a temptation the action is. Get them to hold up the card with the number on it. Use the number 1 for not tempted at all and 5 for very tempted.

4. Talk about each temptation after the family has rated it. Notice that some temptations are harder to resist for some people than for others.

Submerge Yourself in Prayer

Dear God,
I know I can be tempted to do the wrong thing. Thank You for giving me a way out when I am tempted. I want to remember to do the right thing. Give me strength to make good choices that honor You. Amen.

Creator Knows Best

Those who seek the LORD will not lack
any good thing.—Psalm 34:10

Maybe a little more cocoa, and a few more strawberries, and I think it will be perfect," I thought aloud. I was making a special birthday cake for my mom. My son was in the kitchen watching me cook and said, "Mom, where's the recipe? I want to help you make it! I know how to follow directions."

Well, the problem was, I didn't have a recipe! The cake was something I came up with and was making for the first time. "Buddy," I explained, "I'm afraid I don't have a recipe for you to follow."

Tucker looked confused. "But, Mom, then how do you know what else you need to add to the cake to make it good?"

How does God know what I really need when sometimes I don't even know what to ask for?

"Well, I guess because I'm the one who made up the recipe. I know what I want it to look and taste like, so I make those decisions." I could tell Tucker was thinking about what I said, and then a big smile lit up his face. He said, "When will you make the decision to let us eat it?"

Have you ever wondered how God really knows what you need? Think about the cake I made. I planned what I was going to make, shopped for the ingredients, and made the cake. Since I designed the cake, I knew what it should taste and look like. I knew how much of each ingredient I needed.

Think about who designed and created you. God did! He knows you inside and out. He knows your thoughts before you think them, your actions before you do them, and your future before you've lived it. No one knows you better than God. Since He knows you best, He knows exactly what you need. If you are seeking to do God's will and are following Him, He will make sure you have what you need.

Think-Deep Answer of the Week:

God created you, and He always knows
exactly what you need.

Diving Deep
into God's Word

Psalm 139:1—Why does God know you well?

Psalm 139:2—What kinds of things does
God know about you?

Psalm 84:11—Why is it amazing that
God chooses to give you good things?

Psalm 139:4—Why do the words you think matter to
God as much as the words you say out loud?

Psalm 139:17—How does it make you feel when
you really think about how God knows you so
well that He knows your every need?

Chart Your Course

1. Think about how many needs you have in a day (breakfast, clothes, soap, a ride to school, and on and on) and write them down in a numbered list. Invite a family member to guess how many things you listed. Help them guess by telling them if it is higher or lower until they get it right.

2. Ask your family members to act or draw some of their different needs and then take turns guessing those needs.

3. Discuss the difference between a want and a need, and decide which category the things you have listed belong in.

4. Spend time thanking God for knowing what you really need.

Submerge Yourself in Prayer

Dear God,
You know me best, and You love me no matter what. Thank You for providing everything I need. Help me remember that You always know what's best for me.
Amen.

This Way or That Way?

A man's steps are determined by the LORD, so how can anyone understand his own way?—Proverbs 20:24

Next time you're at the beach, the amusement park, or the zoo, take a look around at the parents keeping up with their toddlers. I know I've seen plenty of parents actually running after their little kids! Dad will be trying to catch up with one child who is chasing a bird this way, while Mom is trying to grab the other child from running the other way.

Do you remember being carried around when you were little? How about when you were two or three, and you could walk, but you would get tired after a while? Your mom or dad probably spent some time chasing you, carrying you, and pushing you in a stroller.

Think-Deep Question of the Week:
How do I know which way to go in life?

Now that you are older, your parents don't have to carry you places or chase you anymore. You have control over where you walk, how fast you walk, and when you stop walking, right? But just because you can walk on your own doesn't mean you don't still need guidance and direction from your parents. They know what is best for you and know the things you need to do to have a good life.

God knows the plan He has for your life. He wants you to make the right choices, and He gives you the power to do so. You can learn how to follow God and choose the right path by reading your Bible and praying to God.

Do you trust Him with your steps? Do you pray and ask God to show you what to do and where to go? If you do, great! If not, you can change that right now! Talk to God and tell Him that you want to know Him and follow Him. Ask Him to show you the way. He always will!

Think-Deep Answer of the Week:

God has a plan for you and knows which way you should go in life. Follow His path!

Diving Deep into God's Word

Proverbs 16:9—How do you think things turn out when you know the right thing to do, but you choose to do something different?

Proverbs 19:21—Why is God's plan what's best for your life?

Jeremiah 10:23—Why should you let God choose your steps?

Psalm 37:23—How does it make God feel when you choose to follow His steps?

Proverbs 20:24—Why is it okay if you don't know everything about your future?

Chart Your Course

1. Use your feet to measure several distances in your house, such as the distance from your room to the kitchen, your room to the bathroom, and the back door to the front door. (Walk with your feet toe-to-heel to get your most accurate count.)

2. Invite other family members to measure the same distances with their feet and compare their measurements to yours. Were the numbers the same or different?

3. Everyone's path might look different, just like it takes each member of your family a different number of steps to get to each room. But God wants all His children to come to Him.

4. Discuss this week's Think-Deep Question: "How do I know which way to go in life?" Talk about how God created you and how His plan for your life and your steps is best. You can't compare your steps to others' because God chose to make each person unique.

Submerge Yourself in Prayer

Dear God,
Sometimes I don't want to listen to You, and I try to do my own thing. I know You have a plan for me. Help me trust You with my steps. I want to realize I don't have to compare the plan for my life with anybody else's.
Amen.

Food Is Falling!

The LORD spoke to Moses. "I have heard the complaints of the Israelites. Tell them: At twilight you will eat meat, and in the morning you will eat bread until you are full. Then you will know that I am Yahweh your God."—Exodus 16:11-12

The Israelites were tired of traveling. Yes, they had been freed from slavery, but they were hungry! The travelers were grumbling and unhappy now that they were in the desert. God sent a message to give to the people through Moses. God wanted the people to know He heard their cries and He planned to answer them with food. In fact, God promised to feed the Israelites with meat at night and bread, or manna, in the morning. Then God provided!

God knew the people would need help getting food in the desert. So God sent bread every day, but He gave them specific instructions. He told the people they should gather only what they needed for one day.

Think-Deep Question of the Week:

How did God provide for His people in the Old Testament?

Why did God say that? He wanted the people to trust Him to give them what they needed every single day. Some people did not listen to His instructions, and they took more manna than they needed. But that food spoiled and wasn't any good the next day. God made good on His promise. God provided for the people exactly what they needed, when they needed it, and how they needed it.

The Israelites had to fully depend on God to send them food every day. Can you imagine your food dropping out of the sky every morning? Doesn't that sound a little crazy? God repeatedly gives examples in the Bible of Him meeting the needs of His people. When you choose to obey God, He promises to provide for your needs like He provided for the Israelites who were wandering around in the desert. God probably isn't going to rain down your next roast beef sandwich from the sky, but you can choose to have faith that God will take care of you.

God sent the Israelites food by having manna fall from the sky and providing quail for meat.

Diving Deep into God's Word

Exodus 16:32—Why did the Israelites choose to obey God's commands? How did it benefit them?

John 15:7—What does God ask you to do for Him to receive His blessings?

Exodus 16:8—How does God's care for the Israelites give you the faith to trust Him in your life?

Exodus 16:20—How does the story of the Israelites help you understand the importance of following God's commands exactly?

Exodus 13:21—How does God provide for you in ways beyond food and drink, like He did for the Israelites?

Chart Your Course

1. Choose a favorite recipe to make with your family. It can be a simple snack, a meal, or something you mix up from a box. What you make is up to you!

2. While you are enjoying the food you prepared, invite a family member to read all of Exodus 16. Listen for things you hadn't heard about the story before.

3. Talk with your family about how God provided for the Israelites and the consequences for not following God's directions.

4. Discuss the answer to the Think-Deep Question.

Submerge Yourself in Prayer

Dear God,
Thank You for showing me different ways You provide for people. I know sometimes I don't do things like You ask, and I'm sorry. Help me remember the story of how You gave food to the Israelites. I know You will take care of me too.
Amen.

Surprised by the Supply

And my God will supply all your needs according to His riches in glory in Christ Jesus.—Philippians 4:19

Have you heard about the fire at the elementary school?" read the text my mom sent me late one night. She then told me that the school my dad, aunts, uncles, friends, and I had gone to many years ago was on fire. Soon, I located pictures on the Internet of the devastating fire. It was just a few weeks before school was to start so teachers had already begun to decorate and prepare their rooms. School supplies and materials that teachers—many of them friends I grew up with—had collected over the years and bought with their own money had been destroyed.

Firefighters traveled from all over the area to fight the fire. But they couldn't save the building. Where would the children go to school?

Think-Deep Question of the Week:
When life surprises you, how does God still take care of you?

What would teachers use to help them learn when all their supplies were gone? The community had so many questions and no answers. Soon a plan was in place. A prayer service was held for the community. Then donations began to pour in from people in the community and in different states who wanted to help! Classrooms were created, and so many donations arrived—books, crayons, paper, items for learning centers, and more—that a place had to be designated just to keep them all! By the time school started, teachers and students had places to go and the things they needed!

Does the way you respond to sad and scary situations matter? Yes! The fire was a tragedy for the community, but the way the community responded was a victory. Did you know that absolutely nothing surprises God? It is impossible to do! God knows exactly what is happening all the time. When something happens in your life that you didn't see coming, ask God for help. Then don't be surprised when God provides for your needs above and beyond what you asked! God knows your needs before you do; ask Him and He will provide!

God is never surprised by what happens in your life. He will meet your needs.

Diving Deep into God's Word

Psalm 23:1—What needs does God say He won't meet?

2 Corinthians 9:8—If you are doing God's work, will He provide for you beyond your needs?

Philippians 4:19—Does God have everything necessary to meet your needs?

Psalm 34:10—How does it make you feel to know God wants you to have good things and that He can provide for you?

Colossians 4:2—Why do you think God allows you to ask Him for things through prayer that He already knows you need?

Chart Your Course

1. Talk about how God sometimes uses you and your family as part of His plan to help others who have had a difficult time.

2. Pray and ask God to help you think of a person or organization that needs help right now.

3. Ask God to help you find a way to help. Remember, helping others can be a simple task, such as visiting an older woman who just needs some company, baking some cookies for your local firefighters and thanking them for keeping you safe, or pulling weeds for a neighbor who's sick. Helping does not have to cost a lot of money! You may provide the gift of time, work, or service.

4. As a family, decide whom you will help and the best way to do so. Develop a plan, and put it into action this week!

Submerge Yourself in Prayer

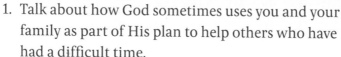

Dear God,
You know everything about me—what I'm thinking and what I'm about to say. I want to trust You and quit worrying about things. I know You are going to take care of for me.
Amen.

A Claustrophobia Lesson

"You will know the truth, and the truth will set you free."
—John 8:32

As my friends and I moved higher and higher up the St. Louis Arch, I noticed my heart began to beat faster and faster. I didn't know I was afraid of small places until I was inside a small, egg-shaped object with several friends. I couldn't wait to be free from the traveling capsule. I just needed some room to breathe! The view was spectacular, but I was ready to get back on the ground.

Have you ever been in a small space—maybe in an elevator with lots of people—and found yourself relieved when you finally reached your destination and were free? Doesn't freedom feel great? There's a much greater feeling of freedom that I hope you'll feel as well—the freedom that comes from understanding the sacrifice Jesus willingly made for you. Knowing this truth about Jesus can set you free. You might be thinking,

Think-Deep Question of the Week:
Why do I need to learn more about Jesus?

I'm not in jail and don't need to be freed! I'm just a kid, remember? Even though you might not be old enough to go to prison, you are old enough to commit sin—something that is wrong and isn't pleasing to God. When you choose to sin, you are held responsible for the sin. You should have to "pay" for what you've done. But because of Jesus' sacrifice, you have the opportunity to have your sins paid in full.

Jesus paid the price for your sins. No, He didn't get out His wallet and give a bunch of money to someone and say, "That ought to cover it!" He did way more than that. Jesus gave His life so you don't have to give yours. Because of Jesus' sacrifice, you can be set free from your sins. You can choose to admit you've committed sins, to believe Jesus died on the cross to save you from those sins, and to confess Jesus as Savior and Lord. When you recognize this truth, pray, and ask God to forgive you, you are free! Isn't that great news? God wants you to be free, and He also desires for you to tell others how to be free as well. Who do you know who needs to hear about the truth that will set them free?

The more you know about Jesus, the more you can live a life that pleases Him.

Diving Deep into God's Word

John 1:17—Why is it important to recognize that Jesus is the truth? How can you explain that to someone who doesn't know much about Jesus?

John 8:36—Why is Jesus the one who can set you free?

Romans 6:18—What kinds of things does Jesus set you free from?

Romans 6:22—What things does Jesus' freedom give you?

Galatians 5:13—What can you do once you understand and accept the freedom you receive from Jesus?

Chart Your Course

1. Invite everyone in the family to think of a subject he or she knows a lot about but the rest of the family might not. (Suggestions include a sport, a movie or television show, or a specific school subject.)

2. Now ask each family member to choose five things to share about the subject. They can be true or false. The other family members will guess if the information is true or false by making the letter shape with their arms, either arms straight out to represent the letter T for "true" or both arms perpendicular on one side to represent F for "false."

3. Talk about how difficult it was to know what was true or false when you didn't know much about the subject.

4. Use your discussion to help you answer today's Think-Deep Question. Why is it important for you to know and tell others the truth about Jesus?

Submerge Yourself in Prayer

Dear God,

Thank You for allowing me to be free even when I know I won't ever deserve it. I want to learn more about Jesus. Help me understand and tell others about the truth that Jesus can set them free. Amen.

The Danger Zone

The Israelites went through the sea on dry ground, with the waters like a wall to them on their right and their left.—Exodus 14:22

Maybe you've heard of the different plagues God sent to Egypt to convince Pharaoh to let the Israelites, who were being held as slaves, go free. God kept sending all sorts of awful things like frogs and hail to show the Pharaoh His power was greater than the Pharaoh's. He even made the sky go completely dark. Did Pharaoh listen? Yes, but only after ten plagues! Finally, Pharaoh agreed to let the Israelites go free. But then he changed his mind and sent his soldiers to capture the Israelites again!

Can you imagine what the freed slaves thought? I can see them thinking, *Are you kidding me? First the answer was yes, and now it's no?* The Egyptian army chased the Israelites to the Red Sea. There was no way to cross the sea to get away from the soldiers. This wasn't a small stream they could jump across, and there was no bridge. There was nothing they could do except to trust God to take care of them.

Moses raised his staff in the air, and the sea split in two. Take a look at Exodus 14:22 and see what the land was like between the two wall-like bodies of water. It was dry! Seconds before, water had covered the ground. Now it was completely dry. Not only did God provide a way for the Israelites to escape, but He also gave them a clean escape. When the Egyptians tried to follow the Israelites, the sea walls came crashing down and swept the Egyptians away.

God provided for the Israelites when they needed protection. Sometimes God has a plan that you may not understand. He wants you to trust in Him and in His promises. God doesn't break His promises. He promises to take care of you, and He will. His plan is always best.

Think-Deep Answer of the Week:

God will be with you when you are in danger.
You can always call out to Him for help.

Diving Deep into God's Word

Psalm 46:1—How is God able to
be your safe place?

Psalm 121:8—Why should you consider God as your guard?

2 Thessalonians 3:3—Why is it good to remember that God
promises to strengthen you, be faithful, and protect you?

Deuteronomy 31:6—Why is it important to know God never fails?

2 Corinthians 12:9—How do you think God
feels about you needing His help?

Chart Your Course

1. Gather a small pan or plastic container, a paint-brush, red food coloring, and heavyweight paper. Place water in the container.

2. Allow your family members to take turns trying to separate the water just like the Red Sea was separated in today's devotion. Challenge family members to use only their hands.

3. Discuss with your family how separating the water is impossible for you to do, and talk about the answer to today's Think-Deep Question.

4. Put some red food coloring in the water, dip the paint-brush in the water, and paint the phrase "God is my Protector" on the heavyweight paper.

Submerge Yourself in Prayer

Dear God,
You are the ultimate Protector! Thank You for taking care of me. When I get scared, help me remember You are always there for me.
Amen.

Chapter 4

Navigating the Waters: Jesus Knows My Purpose

Submarines don't just dive to the bottom of the ocean for fun. They are usually on a mission! The sub might be out to protect land or people, or it could be on an important exploratory assignment. Each person on board knows his role for carrying out the mission at hand. Did you realize you have a mission too? That's right; Jesus has a purpose specifically for you. Let's chart a course right into God's Word and discover your special mission.

Prayer on the Court

Sing to the Lᴏʀᴅ, all the earth.
Proclaim His salvation from day to day.
—1 Chronicles 16:23

May everything we do on and off the court today point people to You, God. In Jesus' name I pray, Amen.." Allie finished her prayer and looked at her teammates. "Y'all ready to play?" she asked with a big grin on her face. The girls' basketball team huddled together and shouted, "One, two, three! Play hard! Can't lose!" before the starting players lined up for the tip-off.

The game was a close one, but the Lady Tigers beat the Clinton Arrows by three points. As Allie's team was celebrating the victory, Caroline looked a little puzzled.

"What's up, C? You don't look too excited about our win," Allie said.

Think-Deep Question of the Week:
What can I do to glorify God?

"Oh, I'm happy. I'm just confused about something you said before the game," explained Caroline. "What did you mean when you said you wanted us to point people to God? I thought we played basketball to win."

Allie explained, "The Bible says that everything we do should bring glory to God. That means that I want to thank God for all the awesome things He has given me, and I want to always do my best and act like Jesus. So whether we win or lose, I want to play fair, be kind, and be a good example to others. Every choice I make, on and off the court, either points people toward God or away from God.

"Hey, why don't you come to Bible class with me this Sunday, C? Mrs. Dawn, our teacher, is great. We'll probably talk about what it means to glorify God in what we do, including basketball!" Allie shared.

Caroline smiled. "Sounds like I can't lose!"

Think-Deep Answer of the Week:

You can glorify God in your life through the things you say and do that are good and pleasing to God.

Diving Deep into God's Word

Isaiah 42:12—Why do you think God wants you to give Him glory?

Isaiah 12:5—What do you see and experience that you think God made glorious?

Psalm 96:1—How can you glorify God?

Psalm 98:1—Why is it important for you to choose to glorify God?

Psalm 115:1—Is it easier to glorify God when you realize He will *always* love you?

Chart Your Course

1. Make a glowing window cling to help you remember to glorify God in what you say and do.

2. Ask a parent to help you gather the following supplies: glow-in-the-dark paint (you can find this in the craft section of most stores), washable white glue, wax paper, and a small disposable bowl and spoon.

3. Decide what shape you want to make to help you remember to glorify God. Some ideas are a star, a sun, or a candle.

4. In the bowl, mix a small amount of glow-in-the-dark paint with the glue. Then use your finger to draw the shape on the wax paper, and let it dry.

5. Peel the dried glue off the wax paper and place it on a window at night. When you see your window cling glowing, it will remind you to glorify God each day.

Submerge Yourself in Prayer

Dear God.
You've done many amazing things for me. Thank You for the beautiful world I live in. I want to glorify You in everything I do. I want to be a good example for others to follow. Help me show others Your love.
Amen.

A Starry Night

**Yahweh is great and is highly praised;
His greatness is unsearchable.—Psalm 145:3**

When's the last time you really looked up at the sky on a clear night? I mean, *really* looked? It can be amazing, can't it? After a night of crab hunting recently, my family took a moment to stare at the stars. They were beautiful! I could hear my son trying to count them. "One, two, three . . ." he said.

"You can't count all those stars, Will! You'll be out here all night, right, Mom?" Reed said.

As I sat on the beach taking in the beautiful heavens, I realized Reed was right. The stars seemed to go on forever. I could never begin to count all of them in the sky or take in all the beauty of God's creation.

Psalm 145:3 says God's "greatness is unsearchable." What do you think that means? It means that God's greatness is so big, so vast, so grand,

Think-Deep Question of the Week:

Why should I praise God?

nothing can contain it! The New Living Translation of Psalm 145:3 says God's greatness cannot be measured. God's greatness is so large you can't understand it. God's greatness is so grand there aren't even words to describe it.

Does it blow you away to think that God's greatness is so huge that no one can explain it and nothing can contain it? The good news is that even though you cannot understand how great God is, you *can* praise Him for His greatness. You can recognize that God is great and that no one on earth will ever compare to God's greatness. You should praise God because He deserves it. In fact, you were designed to praise Him; it's part of your purpose! No one else has or will ever be able to come close to deserving the amount of praise God does. Praise His name forever and forever.

Think-Deep Answer of the Week:

You should praise God because He is greater than anything you can imagine.

Diving Deep into God's Word

Psalm 69:30—What are some ways you can praise God?

Psalm 29:11—How does knowing how great God is make you feel about praising Him?

Psalm 28:7—How do you think God treats people who love and praise Him?

Psalm 33:6—How did God create the stars in the sky, and why would this make you want to praise Him?

Psalm 145:2—How often should you praise God?

Chart Your Course

1. Play a game of "I Can't" with your family. Each family member thinks of a statement that begins with "I can't" and finishes it with something he or she cannot do. If another family member can do the task, that person gets a point.

2. Here are a few ideas to get you started: "I can't rub my stomach and pat my head at the same time!" "I can't say my ABCs backward in less than a minute." "I can't tell a joke without laughing." "I can't count all the stars in the sky."

3. Add up the number of points each family member made.

4. Finish by having each person say something God can do because He is so great. Here's an example: "I can't know how many animals live in the ocean, but God does!"

Submerge Yourself in Prayer

Dear God,
You are more amazing than anyone can even explain!
Thank You for being so great. I want to praise You for who You are and what You've done for me.
Amen.

Working for the Lord

Whatever you do, do it enthusiastically, as something done for the Lord and not for men.—Colossians 3:23

I can't do this! It's way too hard. I quit!" Tatum stormed off the tennis court. Sydney and Gabrielle looked at one another and shook their heads. Tatum was the newest member of the tennis team, and she was a natural tennis player. She had played in a recreational tennis league for a few years, and now Tatum was a part of their school team. The only problem was, Tatum had a unique serve, and the coach wanted her to learn the proper technique. Tatum was getting the hang of it, but she needed some more practice.

Sydney and Gabrielle talked and decided to encourage their new teammate. "My serves would hit the net almost every time when I began to play tennis," Gabrielle explained to Tatum. Sydney nodded. "One day I

Think-Deep Question of the Week:

Why should I work hard?

practiced volleying so many times I could barely lift my arm the next day. We all have to work hard to get better. It takes practice."

Tatum still wasn't buying it. "What's the point, anyway?" Tatum asked, and muttered under her breath, "It's just a silly game. It's not like we are playing at Wimbledon."

Gabrielle and Sydney laughed but then got serious. Sydney looked at Tatum and said, "No, we aren't at Wimbledon. We may never play on those courts. But we are still called to do our very best. Remember at VBS last summer when we learned that Jesus wants us to work hard at whatever we do, whether that's playing sports or taking a test or obeying our parents' rules? My goal is to be a good example for others to see Jesus in me. I want to play like Jesus is watching. I always want to do my best because that makes God happy. Now, let's get back out there. I could use the practice."

"You're right," Tatum said. "Can we all say a prayer together before we play? I want to ask God to help me work hard and do my best too!"

Work hard because everything you do
is for God.

Diving Deep into God's Word

2 Chronicles 31:21—What things do you think
God wants you to work hard at doing?

Proverbs 14:23—What are some things you do
to avoid working hard?

Proverbs 20:13—What kind of message would sleeping all
day send to God about how you feel about hard work?

Colossians 3:17—Are there things you do that God
doesn't care about?

1 Corinthians 10:31—What does working hard
allow you to give to God?

Chart Your Course

1. Do you have a project, chore, or task you've been putting off or haven't completed because you knew it would be hard work? (This could be in your home, in your community, at school, or through your church.)

2. Talk with your parents about your idea. If you can't come up with something, ask them for a special job to complete.

3. Set a goal of when to complete the project and pray about it. Memorize Colossians 3:23.

4. Carry out the project. As you do, recite Colossians 3:23 aloud or softly to yourself. Focus on doing the job well and with a good attitude. Thank God for allowing you to work for Him.

Submerge Yourself in Prayer

Dear God,
I know I've complained before about doing work. I'm sorry.
Help me remember Colossians 3:23 each time I have a hard chore I don't want to do. I want to have a good attitude, and I want to give You glory through my actions.
Amen.

Week 33

Money Mix-Up

> For the love of money is a root of all kinds of evil,
> and by craving it, some have wandered away from the faith
> and pierced themselves with many pains. —1 Timothy 6:10

Do you know what a "chester drawers" is? That's what I used to call a "chest of drawers"! In Spanish class at school one day, I saw a piece of furniture labeled "chest of drawers" and realized I had been saying the wrong words! Maybe something like that has happened to you before. You thought you knew what something was, or you thought you had memorized the words to your favorite song, and then you find out you were wrong!

Sometimes people get confused about what the Bible says too, or they don't remember the words correctly. The words from 1 Timothy 6:10 are

Think-Deep Question of the Week:

How does God want me to feel about money?

often misquoted. Some people think that this verse says, "Money is the root of all evil." But read the verse again. It doesn't say that, does it? The verse says, "The *love of* money is a root of all kinds of evil." Why does it matter that people say the verse wrong? Because it changes the meaning!

God knows money matters. He knows you use money to buy food, clothes, and the things you need. You have to have money! What God doesn't want you to do is love money more than you love Him. God says that thinking about money too much is a bad idea. If you think about something more than God, it may become more important to you than God. God is a jealous God. He wants to be the very most important part of your life. If you find yourself thinking about money too much, ask God for help!

God wants you to love Him much more than you love money.

Diving Deep into God's Word

Psalm 62:10—Why do you think God doesn't want you to think about money all the time?

Proverbs 15:27—A bribe is when you give someone money so that they will do something dishonest for you. How does God feel about things like bribes?

Matthew 6:19—What are some things God says might happen to money?

Mark 4:19—How could having too much money cause you problems?

1 Timothy 6:9—What might happen to people who only think about making money?

Chart Your Course

1. Play a game called "Say What?"

2. Think of something silly to say and then hold your tongue (literally) while you say it.

3. Take turns saying your silly sentences and let your family members guess what has been said.

4. Discuss how easy it is to misunderstand what someone is saying. Understanding what the Bible says about money is very important.

Submerge Yourself in Prayer

Dear God,
Thank You for always providing for me. I know I will need money to buy things. Help me know how to use my money in a smart way. Help me not think about money more than I should.
Amen.

You're Never Too Young

Let no one despise your youth: instead, you should be
an example to the believers in speech, in conduct,
in love, in faith, in purity.—1 Timothy 4:12

"Those are my sea turtle socks! Aunt Candace gave them to me!"
Caroline yelled.

"Well, I found them first, so I am going to wear them," shot back Leah,
Caroline's little sister, who already had them on her feet.

"Dad!" both girls yelled at the same time.

Dad listened to both sides of the story. Before he could decide who got
to wear the socks, Caroline raised her hand. "I have an idea!" Her dad
looked a little unsure at first but agreed to listen to her. "They are my
socks, but what if I wore one of the socks and I let Leah wear the other
one? That way we both would be happy. What do you think, Leah?"

Leah thought about it for a minute, then she started to smile. "I like that
idea a lot! Let's go pick out another pair to each wear one of those too!"

Think-Deep Question of the Week:
How important is it that I make good choices?

Caroline and Leah walked away smiling, and their dad stood there scratching his head.

"I guess I solved that problem!" he said to himself.

What would you have done if you were Caroline? The socks were hers, so she could have made the choice to wear them. She knew her sister wanted to wear them as well. Caroline chose to share. She made the choice to be kind to her little sister. Instead of getting angry and ripping the socks off Leah's feet, she chose to be an example.

You have a choice too. Whether you are five years old or twelve years old, God wants you to be a good example for others to follow. Sometimes making a good choice will be easy, and other times you may have to ask God to help you make the right decision. God wants you to ask for help when you need it! Making wise choices about the friends you choose, the way you treat your parents, and how you react when people aren't nice to you are just a few ways to show others how God wants you to live.

You are never too young to make good choices, and every choice you make matters to God.

Diving Deep into God's Word

John 13:14-15—Who is the best example to follow?

Philippians 3:17—How can you learn more about how to make good choices?

Isaiah 30:21—How do you know how to make the best decisions?

Titus 3:8—What are some reasons it is important to be a good example for others?

I Peter 5:3—Why isn't there a certain age when you suddenly have to start making good choices?

Chart Your Course

1. Ask a parent to help you find some old photos of you and your family. Maybe you can find them in a photo album or saved on a phone or computer.

2. Guess the age of each person in the pictures and use sticky notes to record the ages.

3. Check the dates of the pictures, and figure out how old each person really was, and how many years ago the pictures were taken.

4. Discuss different ways you are setting a good example for others to follow right now, how you did it in the past, and how you can in the future.

5. Choose one way to really focus on setting a good example for others in the next week. Choose an idea such as smiling at people you meet.

Submerge Yourself in Prayer

Dear God,
I want to be a good example for others in the choices I make. Help me remember that it doesn't matter how old I am: I am still important to You.
Amen.

Rest Well

Therefore, a Sabbath rest remains for God's people. For the person who has entered His rest has rested from his own works, just as God did from His. Let us then make every effort to enter that rest, so that no one will fall into the same pattern of disobedience.—Hebrews 4:9-11

God honors hard work, but does that mean you are never supposed to take a break? If you read Genesis 2:2, you'll find out the answer. After six days of creating the world, God chose to rest. Did God need to rest? No. Did God have to get a good eight hours of rest each night? No. So, why did God choose to rest when He didn't have to? (Was it kind of like how you may have felt as a preschooler when your parents tried to make you nap when you didn't feel tired?) God wanted to set a good example for you. God wanted you to see that hard work is important, and so is rest.

How busy are you? Think back to the last five days and what you have done. When you begin to list everything—chores, sports, lessons,

Think-Deep Question of the Week:

Why is rest important?

hanging out with friends—you will begin to realize you have been involved in a lot of different activities. Your body needs rest, and I am not talking about just the sleep you get at night.

When you work hard, you will know when your body needs to rest. Rest is a reward for work! Recognizing the need to slow down is important. Rest can include you and other family members gathering in the family room for an afternoon to talk, to hear about what's happening with each other, and to enjoy each other's company. Rest can be sitting outside on your porch swing and watching the clouds move around the sky. Recently, my rest included a few moments sitting on a beach chair, watching the waves crash on the shore. God designed your life to include rest.

When you have the opportunity to rest, enjoy that time with your family, knowing that even in relaxing you are honoring God!

God wants you to rest so that you can take care of your body and spend time with Him.

Diving Deep into God's Word

Matthew 11:28-30—What does God promise to those who are tired?

Psalm 4:8—What are some good things about getting rest?

Mark 6:31—Why is it important to take a break from the busyness of your life and rest?

Exodus 20:8-11—Who does God say should rest on the Sabbath?

Psalm 62:1-2—Where can you go to find rest?

Chart Your Course

1. Give each family member a piece of paper and pencil. Ask everyone to write down a guess of how much time he or she spends each week (1) in the car, (2) working or being busy, and (3) resting. Talk about the numbers you wrote down and whether those numbers reflect enough rest time.

2. Challenge your family to a rest period. Set a timer for ten minutes, and then spend the time together! You can choose to talk, play worship music, or sit in silence, but make the time about focusing on being together.

3. Brainstorm ways for your family to spend more downtime together—to relax, laugh, and share family devotions. Make a plan to commit to at least one time of rest together a week.

Submerge Yourself in Prayer

Dear God,
Thank You for creating the world. Thank You for making rest important. Help me remember that when everything seems busy, I can find rest in You.
Amen.

A To-Do List

This saying is trustworthy. I want you to insist on these things, so that those who have believed God might be careful to devote themselves to good works. These are good and profitable for everyone.—Titus 3:8

Have you ever made a to-do list? You know, where you list different things you need to do and then check them off when you are finished? Maybe you've noticed your mom or dad doing this. When you finish the list, you can throw it away because you've completed it.

Think about doing "good works" for God. How long should that list be? What kind of things should be on the list? When can you stop doing good things? What if someone else does more good works than you? Does that mean God likes that person more?

Read through Titus 3:8 one more time, and you will notice some of the answers to these questions. The verse says that when you love God, you choose to do good things for Him because you *want* to do those things. Being devoted means that you want to do something with your whole heart and you never want to stop. The list won't end, because there are always things to do to please God, like being kind to your friends and family, helping people who are sad or hurting, making good choices, and telling the truth.

How do you know what you should do for God? Ask Him! Read your Bible, and be sure to check out Diving Deep into God's Word to discover some specific things God says you can do to please Him.

Although it is important to do good things because you love God, you cannot earn God's love, and He will never love you more or less based on what you do. And you cannot compare what you do for God to what someone else does. Save your to-do list for something else, and focus on making choices that please God because you love Him and you are thankful for all the wonderful things He has done for you.

Doing good works means doing anything that pleases God.

Diving Deep into God's Word

Matthew 6:14—Do you think forgiving someone should be considered a good work?

Matthew 5:16—Why is loving God and others an important part of doing good works?

Titus 2:7—Why is being honest and setting a good example for others important?

Titus 3:14—How can you help others who have bad things happen to them, such as a house fire or a tornado?

1 Timothy 5:10—What is hospitality and how can you show that to others?

Chart Your Course

1. Grab a bag that can be closed with a zipper, such as a duffel bag or an overnight bag. Gather one small item from the bedroom, bathroom, kitchen, living room, and closet, and place the items in the bag.

2. With your family, take turns choosing an item out of the bag and sharing one way to use that object to complete a good work for God. For example, if someone pulls out a toothbrush, he could collect toothbrushes and donate them to a local shelter.

3. Repeat the activity several times using the different items.

4. Remember, there isn't a checklist that can be completed for doing good works. Each person must pray and do good works as God leads them. Good works are things people choose to complete out of devotion and love for God.

Submerge Yourself in Prayer

Dear God,
I want to live my life for You. I want to do things that please You and bring You glory. Help me focus on taking care of others and living my life like Jesus.
Amen.

A Telling Testimony

But I count my life of no value to myself, so that I may finish
my course and the ministry I received from the Lord Jesus,
to testify to the gospel of God's grace. — Acts 20:24

AJ was nervous. Soon the judge would ask her to sit in the witness stand.
Her mom had explained she would have to testify. That word was confusing to AJ, but her mom explained it meant she would tell what she
had seen happen in the wreck. AJ didn't have to worry about getting in
trouble, because she was going to tell the truth. The judge just wanted to
know what she saw.

You may have heard of people testifying before a judge too. This usually
means a person tells what happened and answers questions. Each person
who testifies must first promise to tell the truth.

Think-Deep Question of the Week:
What does it mean to testify about God to others?

The word *testify* in Acts 20:24 means something a little different, but it's still about telling the truth. When you testify about the gospel, you are telling others the good news. Testifying about God means you are excited to share what God has done in your life. You want others to know about God and His love for you and them. You don't have to be in a special place to tell others about Jesus. You can testify during a conversation with your friend. You can testify to a family member. You can even testify to the scuba-diving instructor who is helping you get your gear on!

You testify because you want to tell others about Jesus. It's good news! Every single person in this world has the opportunity to have eternal life with Jesus Christ in heaven forever, so it is important for you to tell them about Jesus and His sacrifice on the cross for them. Who can you tell about Jesus today?

Think-Deep Answer of the Week:

Testifying about God to others means you share about God and how important He is in your life.

Diving Deep into God's Word

Ezekiel 2:7—When people don't want to do what God commands, what should you do?

Psalm 40:10—Why is it important not to hide God's love for everyone?

Jeremiah 26:2—What are important things to tell others about God?

Acts 20:20—When you share about God with others, what things should you tell them about God?

Acts 20:27—What might happen if you didn't tell people about God?

Chart Your Course

1. Talk with your family about ways to testify about God's love with others. Make a list of people you could tell about Jesus.

2. How could testifying be hard? How could it be easy?

3. Write out things you could tell someone about how good God is. What are some ways you could show God's love without using words at all?

4. Pray for the chance to testify!

Submerge Yourself in Prayer

Dear God,

You are amazing. You are the Creator of all things. I want to share about You with others. I want to testify to others about Your love. Give me the courage to tell others about You each day. Amen.

Faith in Action

> In the same way faith, if it doesn't have works, is dead by itself. —James 2:17

Sawyer took one more deep breath, then stepped on the submarine. His family was on vacation and they were going to get to ride on a real submarine. Sawyer was claustrophobic (afraid of closed-in spaces) and was worried about being closed up in the submarine. His dad talked with Sawyer and explained, "You have to have faith that the submarine will keep you safe and dry. You can look at it all day, but eventually you have to believe it is safe and get on the submarine." Sawyer and his dad prayed together, and Sawyer had a fabulous experience on his family's submarine ride.

What would have happened if Sawyer said he had faith the submarine was safe, but he never stepped foot on the submarine? Sawyer proved he had faith, in his dad and the submarine, when he walked onboard. The same is true with faith in Jesus. You can say you have faith all day long, but choosing to put that faith into action is what's important.

In this week's verse, James 2:17, you are being challenged to put your faith into action. Do you believe God's plan is best for you? Then trust Him with your prayer requests. Are you worried about how you will do on a test you've studied for? Ask God for peace, then quit worrying. Are you having a difficult time forgiving a friend who hurt your feelings? Ask God for help, and let it go. Are you worried about your dad who lost his job? Ask God to provide for your family.

Have faith in God. Faith is placing your life in God's hands and allowing Him to lead you. When you trust that God loves you and is going to take care of you, you are putting your faith in action and showing God that you really believe that what the Bible says is true.

You show your faith in God when you follow Him and trust Him.

Diving Deep into God's Word

Romans 10:10—How hard is it to trust and have faith that God is in control?

Galatians 5:6—How can you express faith through love?

Hebrews 11:3—What does your faith in God have to do with how the world was created?

James 2:22—What is something you do that requires faith in God?

James 3:13—What is something you've learned from having faith in God?

Chart Your Course

1. Get two cartons of eggs. Inspect the eggs and replace any with small cracks. Arrange them so that the larger end of each egg is facing up. Place the cartons side-by-side.

2. Predict what might happen if you step on the cartons of eggs while evenly distributing the weight of your feet (one foot on each carton).

3. Talk with your family about who has faith that the eggs won't crack when you step on them. Then, test your faith!

4. With help from family members to steady yourself by holding your hands on either side of you, step evenly onto the eggs. If you follow instructions, the eggs will not crack!

5. You can have faith that the eggs won't crack, but you can't prove your faith until you've placed your feet on the eggs.

6. Talk with your family about the importance of having faith in God and how you can remind yourself and others of your faith.

Submerge Yourself in Prayer

Dear God,
You know everything and made everything and have the power to do anything. I want to put all my faith in You every day. Amen.

Everything for Good

We know that all things work together for the good of those who love God: those who are called according to His purpose.—Romans 8:28

"Mom, I'm sorry I forgot to bring my swimsuit for Mia's party. Will you please bring it to me?" Annslee asked her mom over the phone. Her mom agreed and showed up at Mia's house twenty minutes later.

"You're the best, Mom. Thank you!" squealed Annslee as she ran off to get her suit on and join her friends in the pool.

Annslee was in the pool when she looked up and saw her mom smiling and writing something down for Mia's mom. When her mom walked over to tell Annslee good-bye, Annslee asked, "What were you writing down, Mom?"

Think-Deep Question of the Week:

Can we trust God to work everything out for good?

Her mom leaned in so only Annslee could hear. "I was writing down directions to our church. I asked Mia's mom if her family would like to go with us next week, and she said yes!" Annslee smiled and gave her mom a high five. Maybe forgetting her swimsuit wasn't such a bad thing after all.

Do you ever make a mistake? I sure do! Sometimes I get angry with myself for messing something up. Romans 8:28 is a great reminder that no matter what we do, God works things together for His purpose. He's God, remember? You are going to make mistakes. Ask God to forgive you and ask Him for His help. He knows your heart and He knows when you truly want to follow Him. If your goal is to please God, you don't need to worry. He can take anything that happens in your life and work it out for good, for His glory.

The Bible says God will use everything in your life, even your mistakes, for good if you are following Him.

Diving Deep into God's Word

1 Corinthians 1:9—When you make mistakes, why is it good to remember God is faithful?

1 John 2:3—How might people around you know you are a Christian if you don't tell them?

Romans 11:29—How does it make you feel to know God never has and never will break His promises?

Ephesians 3:11—Why do you think it is important to remember God is eternal?

Ephesians 4:1-3—Why is it important not to give up on yourself when you do make mistakes?

Chart Your Course

1. Look back over this chapter and make a few notes about things you've learned.

2. Think about times God has made something good out of something bad or out of a mistake you have made.

3. Write down a few examples on a piece of paper and decorate it. Place it on the inside of your closet door.

4. Ask God to help you remember that He is good and that He is always using everything for good and His glory.

Submerge Yourself in Prayer

Dear God,

Thank You for sending Jesus to die for my sins. Thank You for loving me no matter how many times I mess up. Thank You for forgiveness. I want to live in a way that pleases You. Show me how to do that.

Amen.

Chapter 5

Exploring the Deep Waters:
Jesus Loves and Accepts Me

Even the most experienced scuba divers sometimes deal with faulty equipment, find themselves in scary waters, or have some unsuccessful dives. But that doesn't mean they won't ever dive again—there's a huge ocean out there to explore!

Throughout your life, you will make some bad choices and sometimes find yourself in scary waters too. But Jesus will always be there to guide you and to love you. His love is greater than even all the water found in an ocean. Jesus loves you, and He sees the entire you, not just what's on the surface!

Learning About Love

> There is certainly no righteous man on the earth who does good and never sins.—Ecclesiastes 7:20

Have you ever felt like someone was so much better than you? Maybe you thought your friend was better at sports, had a fancier house, took better vacations, or had more friends than you. Let's go a step further. Have you ever felt like someone was a better Christian than you?

Maybe your friend goes to church more often than you do. Maybe she can quote lots of scriptures from memory. Or maybe she goes to a private Christian school and you go to a public school. Any of these characteristics might cause you to think someone else is a better Christian than you are.

Think-Deep Question of the Week:

What do I do when I feel like Jesus loves someone else more than He loves me?

The truth is, Jesus doesn't play the comparison game. Jesus doesn't love someone more because of his talents or because of the school uniform she wears or because he prays three times a day to Him and you pray twice a day.

Nothing you can do will make Jesus love you more. Nothing you can do can make Jesus love you less. We all sin, even those of us who seem to be doing things right! Do not worry about what other people are doing for Jesus. Focus on how *you* can show Jesus you love Him, always remembering that He loves you more than you'll ever be able to imagine.

Think-Deep Answer of the Week:

Remind yourself what the Bible says:
Jesus loves everyone the same!

Diving Deep into God's Word

Job 34:19—Why do you think God treats the poor and rich exactly the same?

Romans 2:11—Why do you think God repeats His message about favoritism?

Acts 10:34—Why is it important to understand that God accepts people no matter where they are from and what they can do?

Deuteronomy 10:17—How do you know it's impossible for God to love someone else more or less than He loves you?

Romans 9:14—How does it feel to know that God always treats people fairly?

Chart Your Course

1. Ask your family members to each make a list of the important things they do because they are Christians, such as pray and read the Bible.

2. Take turns sharing one of the ideas from your list. If anyone else also has that on his list, he can make a check mark beside it.

3. Talk about different ways your family members show love for Jesus.

4. Reread Ecclesiastes 7:20 aloud. Discuss with your family why Jesus doesn't love people based on how much they do for Him. Jesus loves everyone equally.

Submerge Yourself in Prayer

Dear God,
Sometimes it is hard not to compare what I do to what other people do. Sometimes I feel like I'm not a good enough Christian. Please help me remember that You are amazing and I don't have to do anything to earn Your love.
Amen.

Love That Lasts Forever

The LORD appeared to him from far away. I have loved you
with an everlasting love; therefore, I have continued
to extend faithful love to you.—Jeremiah 31:3

When Jacob found out that he had won, he was so excited! He was getting
to go on an all-expenses-paid trip to the best water park in the country,
and he could bring his two best friends, Jack and Brian. He couldn't wait
to tell them about the tallest water slide in the world. Right before Jacob
called his friends to share the news, his dad stopped him.

"Jacob, are you sure the trip is totally free?" asked his dad.

"Of course it is, Dad. I've read the whole letter from the water park.
Now all we have to do is decide when we want to go." Jacob picked up
the letter to read the details to his dad. "As long as I call by May 3—wait,

today is June 3. I just got the letter yesterday! How is that even possible? It's got to be wrong!"

Jacob's dad called the water park, and sure enough, the free-trip offer had expired.

It's never fun to find out that time has run out and you aren't going to get something you were hoping for. But one good thing—a great thing, the best thing—never expires. It's God's love! Jeremiah 31:3 tells us how much God loves you and me, and He promises that His love is everlasting. That means no matter what, no matter when, God's love will last forever.

Diving Deep into God's Word

Exodus 20:6—How do you think God feels about those who follow His commandments?

Psalm 25:6—Do you think God has ever stopped showing love to others?

Psalm 89:2—What should you do with the knowledge that God's love has no end?

Psalm 103:17—How long does God's love last?

Luke 1:50—How does it make you feel to know God's love and His mercy never end?

Chart Your Course

1. Grab a balloon, bouncy ball, or basketball. If you only bounce the ball once, how many times do you think it will keep bouncing on its own? Write down your guess, and ask each family member to guess too.

2. Collect the guesses and then complete the experiment to see who guessed the closest without going over. Now repeat the experiment on a different surface. Does the ball or balloon bounce differently on tile or grass or carpet?

3. Talk with your family about why the ball or balloon stopped bouncing.

4. Discuss how the ball is different from God's love. The ball, no matter how many times it bounces, will eventually stop. Point out that God's love will never stop, no matter what you do.

Submerge Yourself in Prayer

Dear God,
Thank You for Your love! Thank You that it never stops.
Help me share Your amazing love with others. Help me remember that You will never stop loving me no matter what happens or what I do.
Amen.

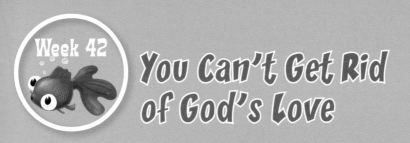

You Can't Get Rid of God's Love

God's love was revealed among us in this way: God sent His One and Only Son into the world so that we might live through Him. Love consists in this: not that we loved God, but that He loved us and sent His Son to be the propitiation for our sins.—1 John 4:9-10

Have you ever heard the saying, "Can't never could"? The saying is often used to help someone see that what they are struggling with is a mental game. Do you know what a mental game is? It's a game that goes on inside your head. That's right! You didn't know there was a game in there, did you? It's true. Your brain is always working, trying to figure things out and to make the best decisions.

The minute you think, *I can't . . .* , you've begun to think in a negative way. Maybe you think you *can't* be loved by God because of things you've done in the past. I know people who think they *can't* be loved by God because they don't always make the best choices in life. I know people who think they *can't* be loved by God because their own family doesn't love them. Can you imagine not feeling loved?

Here's something you need to know: no matter what you have (or haven't) done in your life, and no matter how unloved you feel, you will always be loved by God, even if you don't love Him back. God doesn't love you because you choose to love Him first. The fact is, God's love is something that you can't get rid of even if you tried. So if you are struggling in your thoughts with whether God loves you, remember what the Bible says: God loves you. He always has, and He always will!

Even if you feel like you can't be loved by God,
God still loves you more than you can imagine!

Diving Deep
into God's Word

John 3:16—Why did God send Jesus to earth?

1 John 4:8—What does the Bible mean when
it says that God is love?

1 John 4:9-10—How does God sending Jesus to
earth show you that God loves you?

1 John 4:16—Why do you think it is hard for
some people to believe God loves them?

1 John 4:19—How can you learn to love others?

Chart Your Course

1. Write down the name of each family member who lives in your home (including you) on a separate piece of paper. Invite your family members to write things they love about each person on the papers. Then enjoy reading all the things your family loves about you!

2. Talk about how God loves you more than you can imagine, even more than your family does.

3. Sometimes saying things out loud is more important than you think! Ask each family member to look up one of the following verses: Romans 8:38–39; Ephesians 3:18–19; Psalm 86:15. Read the verses out loud as reminders that God loves you more than anyone else does.

Submerge Yourself in Prayer

Dear God,
Thank You for loving me more than I could ever imagine. Help me remember Your love is always there for me. I want to share Your wonderful love with others too.
Amen.

Remembered No More

> Then I acknowledged my sin to You and did not conceal my iniquity. I said, "I will confess my transgressions to the LORD," and You took away the guilt of my sin. —Psalm 32:5

When you look out over an ocean, you might not be able to see any land. The truth is, if you got in a boat and paddled long enough, you would eventually find land again. So even though land seems far, far away, it is still out there. Sometimes we think that's what God does with our sin. He says that He forgives us, but we worry that maybe it's still out there, that God is keeping a list and all our sins are going to add up to something pretty bad someday. But guess what? The Bible says that when God forgives our sins, He will never again hold them against us. They are gone because they have been paid for by Christ on the cross, and He judges you based on Christ's perfect obedience.

Think-Deep Question of the Week:

How long does God remember my sins?

Maybe you are afraid to admit something to God because you think He will be disappointed or angry or turn His back on you. No matter what you've done wrong, God will forgive you. He isn't keeping a record of how many times you have sinned and what kinds of sins you have committed. When you ask Him to forgive you, He wipes that sin away.

Jesus loves you now, and He always will. Jesus died on the cross to take away your sin. God's forgiveness is always there, waiting for you to ask for it. Once you ask for and receive God's forgiveness, He holds no record of your wrong. Jesus loves you. Ask Him to forgive you and be comforted, knowing that He remembers that sin no more.

Think-Deep Answer of the Week:

God doesn't keep a list of your sins. Once you've asked for forgiveness, the sin is gone.

Diving Deep into God's Word

1 John 1:9—Why is it important for you to understand that God will forgive you of your sins?

Psalm 103:12—How far does God remove our sins from us?

John 8:36—Why does God call you "free" when He forgives you of a sin?

Colossians 3:13—How should you treat others when they mistreat you, knowing God has forgiven you?

Proverbs 28:13—When God promises mercy to those who confess their sins, what does He mean?

Chart Your Course

1. Gather your family. Have each person write a list of sins they have done that week. Let everyone know that no one will see the list. It's just between you and God.

2. Pray silently or as a family, asking God to forgive everything on your lists.

3. Talk about how God forgives and forgets everything on those lists. Then brainstorm funny ways to destroy the lists, like feeding them to a shark, blowing them up with dynamite, or throwing them into a volcano.

4. With your parents' help, actually destroy your lists (cutting them into tiny pieces will work!).

5. Spend some time together praying as a family and thanking God for the gift of forgiveness.

Submerge Yourself in Prayer

Dear God,
I know I mess up and make mistakes. Please forgive me.
Help me remember that You always forgive my sins.
Amen.

Judge Not

Therefore don't judge anything prematurely, before the Lord comes, who will both bring to light what is hidden in darkness and reveal the intentions of the hearts. And then praise will come to each one from God.—1 Corinthians 4:5

Gross! That looks disgusting!" my son Reed said as I placed his dinner on the table.

First, I reminded him it is not polite to complain about the food someone has made for him. Then I said, "Have you tasted it yet?" Reed shook his head no and leaned in to sniff the food. "Before you decide what you think of the food, please taste it," I told Reed. Sure enough, he took a bite and loved it! He even asked for seconds.

What if Reed hadn't tasted the food? He would have decided it tasted bad because of the way it looked. He would have missed the chance to try something new and realize it was yummy.

Think-Deep Question of the Week:

Why is it wrong for me to judge other people?

You shouldn't judge things just because of how they look, but that rule is even more important when it comes to people. Have you ever found yourself judging a person without knowing anything about him? The Bible is clear about how you should treat others. Matthew 7:1 states, "Do not judge." The Bible says that God is the only one who can judge another person's heart. You don't know what is going on in someone's heart. Only God knows that. No matter what a person has done, might have done, or will do, your job isn't to decide how to punish someone for his or her sins. No sin is too great for God to handle.

The good news is you don't have to worry about judging other people's sins. Make your focus in life about pleasing God and showing love to others, and don't judge other people in your life. Treat others with grace and forgiveness, just like God treats you.

God is the ultimate judge, and it's what
He thinks that matters.

Diving Deep
into God's Word

Ecclesiastes 12:14—How does God handle
people who try to hide their sins from Him?

Matthew 7:1—Why is it not a good idea to judge
other people and what they do?

Exodus 14:14—When someone has mistreated you, how difficult
is it to let go of that hurt and realize God is in control?

Hebrews 4:13—Why is it important to remember
that God sees and knows everything?

Revelation 3:19—Who is in charge of disciplining
people who have sinned against God?

Chart Your Course

1. Gather some paper plates or white paper, some crayons or markers, and old magazines.

2. Ask family members to draw or cut out pictures of food to create an amazing meal.

3. Compare all the meals and talk about the similarities and differences between them.

4. Talk with your family about how each of you had a different idea of an amazing meal, but this didn't mean one was any less amazing than another.

5. Discuss with your family how no one's sins—no matter what they are—are considered better or worse to God. It's God's choice how to handle the sin of each person.

Submerge Yourself in Prayer

Dear God,
Help me obey You and not worry about what other people are doing. I want to make You happy.
Amen.

Through God's Eyes

Honor everyone. Love the brotherhood.—1 Peter 2:17

Morgan and Carissa made their way through the lunch line. "Are you really going to sit by Leigh?" Morgan asked with a weird face. "Haven't you heard the rumors about her? Everyone is talking about what a bad reputation she had at her old school. You know she got in lots of fights with people."

Carissa didn't like hearing her new friend Leigh talked about that way. With all the courage she could gather, she responded, "Well, Leigh has been nothing but nice to me. Plus, she's been through a hard time. Her parents divorced, and that's why she's at our school now."

Carissa paid for her lunch, walked straight toward the lunch table, and plopped herself down right beside Leigh. She turned to her friend and said, "So, are you going to the movies with everybody on Friday night to see *Submarines and Sushi*?"

When Leigh looked down nervously, Carissa quickly realized that her new friend had not been invited. So she came up with a different idea.

"Or . . . how about we plan to watch the prequel to *Coral Reef Catastrophe* at my house instead?" Leigh smiled and agreed.

The bell rang, and everyone started rushing around to get back to class. Morgan stopped long enough to roll her eyes at Carissa before dashing down the hall.

Carissa just shook her head. She hoped one day Morgan would ignore the gossip and be kind, but until then, Carissa just needed to focus on loving others the way Jesus wanted her to. No matter what other people said about her friend Leigh, Carissa knew it was God's opinion of Leigh that mattered most.

God wants you to treat everyone with love and respect.

Diving Deep into God's Word

Matthew 7:12—How should you respond to people who treat you unfairly?

Luke 6:31—How do you want to be treated? How well do you treat others?

Matthew 22:39—Why do you think it is easier to love yourself than others sometimes?

Romans 13:10—How does showing love affect people?

James 2:8—What does the Bible say about those who love others?

Chart Your Course

1. Think about the word *reputation*.

2. Make a list of different kinds of reputations people may have.

3. Decide what kind of reputation is pleasing to God.

4. Find and read aloud Philippians 4:8.

5. Ask yourself: What does this verse say I should think about?

Submerge Yourself in Prayer

Dear God,

Help me love all people. I want my reputation to be pleasing to You. I want to treat those around me with kindness and love. Thank You for loving me.

Amen.

Is Seeing Believing?

> Now faith is the reality of what is hoped for, the proof of what is not seen.—Hebrews 11:1

I'll believe it when I see it!" explained my friend. No matter how hard I tried to convince her, Shelby just could not believe I could hold my breath underwater for almost two minutes. Many of my friends had seen me do it and told Shelby I could, but it didn't matter! Shelby had no faith in me. On Sunday afternoon, Shelby came over to swim, and she timed me as I held my breath for almost two minutes. She finally believed me after I proved it to her.

Do you struggle with faith? Check out how faith is defined in Hebrews 11:1. Faith involves believing something without being able to see it for yourself. When you choose to become a Christian, you are showing others the faith you have in Christ, the Savior of the world. After you become a Christian, what happens to your faith? God desires for your faith to grow even larger and stronger.

As you learn more about God, the more your faith grows. What if something has happened to you and you are struggling to believe God can help you? Pray to God and ask for help. You will never physically see the body of Jesus until heaven, so you are exercising your faith by believing Jesus exists. Ask Jesus to help your faith grow, and He will help you!

Here's the good news: you don't have to have all the answers; God does! You can always ask God for help, and He will always help you. When you find yourself struggling with having enough faith, ask God for help and watch Him work. Have faith in God, and watch your faith grow too!

Think-Deep Answer of the Week:

Faith means that you believe in God, even if you can't see Him.

Diving Deep into God's Word

Ephesians 2:8—Why is it important to remember how a person is saved by God?

2 Corinthians 5:7—How do you make decisions about life when you can't tell what will happen in the future?

Hebrews 10:38—How does God feel about people who choose not to live by faith?

Hebrews 10:39—What is a benefit of having faith in God?

1 Peter 1:5—How do you know you are being protected by God's power?

Chart Your Course

1. Gather a cup, a few tablespoons of baking soda, a half cup of vinegar (white or apple cider), and some scrap pieces of paper.

2. Place the baking soda in the cup. Ask each family member to guess if they think pouring the vinegar in the cup will cause the foam to bubble up and over the cup lid. Collect everyone's responses on a piece of paper.

3. Conduct the experiment and see who guessed correctly.

4. Each person believed that their answer was correct. Talk with your family about why they had faith in their answer. Discuss how faith in Jesus is similar and how it is different too.

Submerge Yourself in Prayer

Dear God,

I love You. Help me have faith in You. When I need help, please show me what to do. Let my friends see how important my faith in You is to me.

Amen.

Diving in Deep Water

> What should we say then? Should we continue in sin so that grace may multiply? Absolutely not! How can we who died to sin still live in it? —Romans 6:1-2

The last time I tried to swim to the bottom of the swimming pool, it hurt my ears. The next time I go swimming, I could choose to swim to the bottom of the pool again, but I'm not going to. Do you know why? I already know what will happen, and I've learned not to make the same mistake twice!

When you ask Jesus to forgive you of a sin, He will. So, is it wrong to continue to commit the same sin over and over and keep asking for forgiveness each time? The answer to this question has a lot to do with how you feel about Jesus. When you love Jesus, you want to please Him. You want to do things that honor God and give Him the glory He deserves.

Think-Deep Question of the Week:

Is it okay to keep choosing to sin since God will keep forgiving me?

As a Christian, you also want to learn from the mistakes you make so you can make better choices the next time you are in a similar situation. When you learn from what you've done, it changes what you will choose to do in the future.

The reason you wouldn't repeat the same sin over and over again is that you want to please God. When you love Him, you want to make Him happy by making good choices. When you make a poor decision, you can ask for forgiveness and move on. Focus on loving God and doing things that are good and right. Life will be much better when you are making choices that honor Him!

If you love God, you try to avoid sin because you want to please Him.

Diving Deep into God's Word

Hebrews 6:6—How does committing one sin over and over affect the way a person lives?

2 Peter 1:3-4—Why does loving God help you choose to say no to sin?

2 Peter 2:20—How do you think God feels when you keep doing the same wrong thing?

2 Peter 2:19—When you choose to sin the same way over and over, what are you allowing sin to do to you?

2 Peter 3:18—When you are struggling with a sin, what can God do to help you?

Chart Your Course

1. Challenge yourself and family members to see how many words you can form out of the letters in the words *forgiveness* and *sins*.

2. Compare your list of words with other family members' lists.

3. Talk with your family about how no matter how many times you make a mistake or mess up, God is always there to forgive you if you ask Him to.

4. Work with your family to focus on ways you are honoring God with what you say and do instead of thinking about how many times you have sinned or will sin.

Submerge Yourself in Prayer

Dear God,
I'm so glad You choose to forgive me when I mess up. Thank You for listening to me. I want to make choices that please You, today and every day.
Amen.

Using Your Gifts

But He gives greater grace. Therefore He says: God resists the proud, but gives grace to the humble.—James 4:6

When I first met Carter, he could not stop talking about all the things he was good at doing, which included scuba diving, snorkeling, identifying all the different kinds of fish in the ocean, surfing, and sailing. He talked for ten minutes straight about how good he was at all those things and never asked me one question about myself. His sister was with him, but she didn't say a word until Carter stopped talking. Then I was able to ask his sister what her job was. She quietly told me she helped design space crafts that would land on Mars in the next few years. Impressive, right? Too bad Carter's prideful talk almost kept us from getting to know each other.

Think-Deep Question of the Week:

How does my pride affect me?

Is it wrong to do something well? Absolutely not! God gives each person specific gifts, and God loves to know you are using your gifts for His glory. What's the difference between the two siblings above? One chose to talk a lot about all the things he was good at doing while the other one didn't make a big deal out of her talent.

According to James 4:6, God gives grace to the humble. This means God recognizes people who do not make a big deal, or brag, about their talents and abilities. Remember where those abilities and talents came from? God! God already knows what you are good at doing, because He designed and created you! You don't have to impress God or anyone else. When you focus on serving God, your gifts will shine.

Your pride can keep you from being thankful for all God has given you.

Diving Deep into God's Word

Jeremiah 9:23-24—What do you think God wants people who are rich, strong, and smart to talk to others about?

Philippians 2:3—Why do you think God wants you to treat others as more important than yourself?

Proverbs 18:12—How is humility better to have than pride?

Psalm 10:4—Why is being too prideful dangerous?

1 Corinthians 13:4—Why is it important to realize that love isn't proud or boastful?

Chart Your Course

1. Locate the book *The Rainbow Fish* and read it with your family. (If you don't already own it, check it out from your local library, or you can ask your parents to help you find a recording of someone reading it online.)

2. Discuss the lessons the fish learned in the book. What happened when the fish didn't want to share his fins? What happened to the fish when he let go of his pride?

3. Spend time in prayer with God. Use the prayer below as a way to begin your prayer time.

Submerge Yourself in Prayer

Dear God,
I know what the Bible says about pride, and it's not good to have it. Please help me recognize when I'm being prideful. I want everything I say and do to honor You, not me.
Amen.

Week 49

Dealing with Jealousy

But if you have bitter envy and selfish ambition in your heart, don't brag and deny the truth. Such wisdom does not come from above but is earthly.—James 3:14-15

Beautiful, *smart*, and *rich* are words that describe one family that lives in my community. Everyone in the family always dresses nicely, they have a beautiful home and drive super nice cars, and they take amazing vacations to the beach every year. Do you see why it's easy to be jealous of this family? Who wouldn't want to live that life, right?

Do you struggle with jealousy? Maybe you don't know a family like I just described, but you sure wish you had as many friends as Savannah does. Or maybe you would love to have the latest gaming system that Eli's dad just gave him for no reason at all. You don't even get something that big on your birthday.

Think-Deep Question of the Week:

Why is jealousy a sin?

God knows everything about you. You can't hide your feelings of jealousy from Him. What you *can* do is ask God to take those feelings away. Being jealous of what someone has takes your focus off pleasing God and puts it on another person.

Jesus will never love you more or less because of the jealousy you feel toward other people. But God does want you to focus your attention and your energy on pleasing God and not people. When you find yourself slipping into the distraction of jealousy, call on God! Ask God to help you be thankful for all the wonderful things He has given you.

Jealousy puts your focus on another person instead of on God.

Diving Deep into God's Word

Galatians 5:14-15—What are some possible consequences of being jealous of others?

Job 5:2—How could feelings of jealousy lead to anger?

Proverbs 23:17—How could jealousy of others distract you from God?

1 Peter 2:1-2—When you can put aside jealousy, how will that help your relationship with God?

Romans 5:8—Why is it important to realize Jesus died for you knowing you were a sinner?

Chart Your Course

1. Get a large piece of poster board and a few pens. Ask every family member to take a pen and start writing down or drawing pictures of God's blessings. See if you can cover the whole sheet!

2. Read out loud one of the verses from this week's lesson.

3. Talk about all the things you are grateful for. How can focusing on those things keep you from being jealous of what others have?

Submerge Yourself in Prayer

Dear God,
Thank You for all the blessings You have given me and how much You love me. I know comparing myself and what I have to someone else isn't a good choice. When I begin to feel jealousy toward others, help me realize it and change.
Amen.

Doubts About Diving Deep

Jesus answered them, "I assure you: If you have faith and do not doubt, you will not only do what was done to the fig tree, but even if you tell this mountain, 'Be lifted up and thrown into the sea,' it will be done."—Matthew 21:21

Trae is an underwater welder. Do you know what that is? I didn't either until he explained it to me. He puts on a wetsuit, a super heavy helmet, and his scuba gear. Then he grabs his tools and dives very deep into the ocean. His job is to repair pipes that are broken on oil rigs. Don't ask me how he does it, but he uses fire and heat to weld pipes together so the oil rig continues to run and produce oil like it is designed to do.

What would happen if Trae doubted his equipment was going to work? There's no way he would ever dive into the depths of the ocean if he didn't trust his gear to supply him with oxygen to breathe! In fact, sometimes his dives are so deep that when he comes back to the surface,

Think-Deep Question of the Week:

What if I have doubts?

he has to stay in a compression chamber full of helium (the gas used to make balloons float) to help his body adjust from being so deep in the water! It sounds like pretty serious stuff to me.

Along with being an underwater welder, Trae is a Christian. He's been through some hard times in his life. Through his experiences, he has learned that doubting God isn't helpful. Just like Trae knows better than to doubt his equipment's ability to keep him safe in a dive, he also knows he needs to let go of any doubts he has about God and have faith instead. When he trusts his equipment, he is rewarded with amazing deep-water views of sea creatures. Choosing to let go of doubt in God allows him to grow deep in his faith and see the incredible ways God will use him to bring others to God.

Think-Deep Answer of the Week:

Share your doubts with God. He can help you have faith in Him instead.

Diving Deep into God's Word

James 1:6—Why do you think God describes doubt like a wave in the sea?

Mark 11:22-23—How powerful is faith?

Psalm 62:8—When should you trust in God?

Mark 9:24—What should you say to God if you are dealing with doubt?

John 11:40—What does God promise those who choose to believe in Him instead of doubting Him?

Chart Your Course

1. Ask your family members to think of one thing that's true about themselves and one thing that could be true, but isn't. Here's an example: "I've been deep-sea fishing. I love to go crab hunting." One is true and one isn't!

2. Take turns sharing what you wrote. Everyone else can vote on whether a statement is true or false by saying, "Yep, I have faith in that!" or "I doubt it!" (You could play this game with a group of friends too!)

3. Talk with your family about what things in life are okay to doubt and what things aren't. You can always be sure that everything God has said and done is true and correct.

Submerge Yourself in Prayer

Dear God,
Thank You for loving me. Help me always to trust You completely and never doubt Your power.
Amen.

Measuring Your Progress

And Jesus increased in wisdom and stature, and in favor with God and with people. —Luke 2:52

"**H**ouston, we have a problem!" Ethan said as he walked into the living room wearing a wetsuit that clearly was way too small for him.

"Oh, man! That is so funny!" his friend Cole said and then fell over from laughing. "Exactly whose wetsuit are you wearing? Your little sister's?"

"Ha, ha. Very funny. This is *my* wetsuit! Dad bought it for me for my birthday, and I wore it all last summer while we took classes to be certified scuba divers. I had no idea I grew this much in a year! Looks like I know what I'll be using my Christmas cash on now: a new wetsuit."

Ethan had grown several inches, and he clearly needed a new wetsuit since his old one didn't fit anymore. Although Ethan's physical growth was easily noticed, it was harder to tell if he had grown as a Christian that year as well. Spiritual growth isn't always easy to see or measure.

Think-Deep Question of the Week:

Why do I need to continue to grow as a Christian?

Are you supposed to grow as a Christian? Take a closer look at Luke 2:52 and notice the person mentioned as growing in "wisdom and stature"—it's Jesus! Jesus, sent by God to earth to teach and share the gospel with others, grew from a child to an adult in many good ways.

God loves everyone, and He wants everyone to become a Christian. After you've become a Christian, He wants you to continue to learn from the Bible, study it, and share what you've learned with others. The more you grow as a Christian, the more truth you will discover. What you learn about God in the Bible can teach you how to live a life that God has planned for you. You don't have a spiritual wetsuit you can try on every year to see how much you've grown. So ask yourself: Am I learning and growing more like Christ every day?

Think-Deep Answer of the Week:

Choosing to grow as a Christian is a part of God's plan for your life.

Diving Deep into God's Word

1 Samuel 2:26—How old do you have to be to grow as a Christian?

Psalm 111:10—How does following God's Ten Commandments help your faith become deeper?

Colossians 3:16—Why is praising and worshiping God important?

Exodus 23:13—What can you do to help others see you as a growing Christian?

1 Timothy 4:16—Who can you help as you continue to grow as a Christian?

Chart Your Course

1. Write the name of each of your family members on a separate piece of paper or index card. Ask your family members to write how tall they believe each family member is.

2. Use a tape measure to discover the correct height of each person and compare it to the guesses.

3. Talk with your family about ways to measure how you grow as a Christian. Ask your parents to share ways they've seen Christians grow. If you haven't heard your parents share about how they became Christians, this would be a great time to ask them.

Submerge Yourself in Prayer

Dear God,
I want to grow as a Christian. Show me how. I want to learn more about You.
Amen.

Growing Strong

> I gave you milk to drink, not solid food, because you
> were not yet ready for it.—1 Corinthians 3:2

What would happen if you tried to feed a little baby a double-decker hamburger? The baby wouldn't know what to do with it! Babies don't have teeth to chew food, and babies don't learn how to feed themselves until they are older. Babies begin their lives drinking milk, not eating food. As their teeth come in, their moms begin giving them small bits of soft food to let them taste and learn how to chew. The bigger a child grows, the more nutrients and food he needs to survive and continue to grow into a healthy adult.

No matter how old you are when you make the decision to become a Christian, you are considered a baby. No, you don't have to sleep in a baby bed or eat baby food, but the Bible does say God begins to teach you through His Word. He compares what you learn to milk, just like a baby drinks! The more you learn and grow as a Christian, the more you can understand.

You begin to learn more about God as you pray, study your Bible, choose wise friends, and listen and learn from Christian leaders. The more you surround yourself with people who love God and want to know Him, the more encouraged you will be to do the same! You can choose to spend time learning more about God every single day. Just as your body is changing and growing, so is what you know and understand about the Bible and how God wants you to live.

Ask God to help you learn and grow more as a Christian, and He will! You may read a verse as a young Christian one way, then study it a year later and learn something completely different. You can never study the Bible too much. By praying, studying your Bible, and learning from other Christians, you will grow your faith!

Grow spiritually by praying, studying your Bible, and spending time with other Christians.

Diving Deep into God's Word

Colossians 3:9-10—How should your life change as you grow as a Christian?

1 Peter 2:2—What kind of attitude do you think God wants you to have about being a growing Christian?

Ephesians 4:15—In what area does God most want you to grow?

Romans 5:3-4—When things happen in your life that make you sad or mad, how do you think God wants you to learn from what happened to you?

2 Corinthians 3:18—Why should you be excited about other people growing as Christians too?

Chart Your Course

1. Ask your parents to get you a notebook to use as a journal, or use one you already have at home. Tear out the used pages if you need to.

2. Decorate the front of the notebook. One option is to create an ocean-in-a-bag by filling a zip-top plastic freezer bag with some hair gel and glitter (you want a sturdy and thick bag). Use clear packing tape to reinforce each side, and attach it to the front of the journal.

3. Talk with your family about the experiences you've had with them as you've worked your way through this devotional. Ask them to share their favorite activities, verses, and topics. Make a list in your journal.

4. Use the journal to record your thoughts or the verses you like as you study your Bible. You could also list prayer requests and praises. Use it to help you keep track of spiritual growth too. Remember to date your entries so you know when you wrote in it each time.

Submerge Yourself in Prayer

Dear God,
You have the power to do anything. Thank You for choosing to love me. Thank You for never giving up on me. Thank You for teaching me. Thank You for loving me just like I am. Help me live the best life I can for You.
Amen.

PARENT
Connection

B&H KIDS

Remember: Search me, God, and know my heart;
test me and know my concerns. See if there is any offensive way
in me; lead me in the everlasting way.—Psalm 139:23-24

Read: Read Luke 19:1–10. When the rich tax collector Zacchaeus wanted to see Jesus, the Lord called Zacchaeus by name and joined him for a meal. The people in the crowd complained because Zacchaeus was a sinful man. But Jesus saw Zacchaeus for who he really was underneath—a man in need of salvation. Jesus sees who you really are deep inside too. He knows your heart and your true worth, and He loves you no matter what.

Think:

1. How do you think Zacchaeus felt when he realized that Jesus knew what he was really like inside?

2. Have you ever judged something on the outside (a food, a house, a book) and then realized it was totally different on the inside? Were you disappointed or glad? What can you learn from that mistake?

3. Think about the people you see throughout the week. Are there any people who seem okay on the outside but might be sad or lonely underneath? How can you look below the surface and show love to them?

4. What is the most valuable thing you own? How does it make you feel to know that you are incredibly valuable to Jesus, even though you mess up?

5. Are there some things you don't want Jesus to know about you? You can't hide anything from Him, but you can be sure that He loves you no matter what.

6. List three ways you can get to know who Jesus really is.

Jesus sees. Jesus knows. Jesus saves.